Atlantic Gardening

Peter J. Scott

Illustrations by Michael Walsh

BOULDER
PUBLICATIONS

Library and Archives Canada Cataloguing in Publication

© 2010 Scott, Peter J.

Atlantic gardening : Nova Scotia, New Brunswick, Prince Edward
Island / Peter J. Scott.

Includes bibliographical references.
ISBN 978-0-9809144-8-1

    1. Gardening--Maritime Provinces. I. Title.

SB453.3.C2S36 2010   635.09715   C2010-900695-X

Published by Boulder Publications
Portugal Cove-St. Philip's, Newfoundland and Labrador
www.boulderpublications.ca

Front cover: Sarah Hansen
Layout by Vanessa Stockley, GraniteStudios.ca
Printed in Canada

Newfoundland
Labrador

We acknowledge the financial support of the Government
of Newfoundland and Labrador through the Department
of Tourism, Culture and Recreation.

We acknowledge financial support for our publishing program by the
Government of Canada and the Department of Canadian Heritage through the
Canada Book Fund.

Contents

Introduction

Gardening has been a human endeavour ever since people decided to settle in one place and stabilize their food supply. Today, most gardens are places of recreation, relaxation, and beautification. People enjoy having their own flowers to pick for the house, and their own vegetables, some of which are not available from the grocery store.

This book is intended to explain the basics and some of the details of gardening. It is also written to address some of the peculiarities of gardening on the East Coast of Canada. I once heard of a keen gardener who had spent his working years in Vancouver before retiring on the East Coast. When asked why he had moved, he replied that there was no challenge to gardening in Vancouver. Let us hope that there was not too much here!

The ideal situation would be for potential gardeners to buy a property when they are in robust health and have a cast-iron back with a hinge in it and adequate energy to use it. Soil preparation and modifications of the landscape consume excess energy and work out the frustrations we all encounter as we struggle toward our dotage. Then, we can plant a few bulbs and spread a little compost as the snow settles on the mountain.

There are many approaches to a property, depending upon your interests, but, once the beds have been established, their contents can change. Strawberries may give way to dahlias or prize carrots. That is the joy of gardening. Themes may alter – a pink (flowered) garden may be replaced by a dried flower garden, then by a fragrance garden. Many plants will grow in Atlantic Canada, and, since space is usually limited in the garden, each gardener should move through a list of "must try" plants.

This book will start with terra firma and what a firm foundation – usually bedrock – we have in some areas. Soil preparation is critical to success in gardening and as much effort as possible should be expended in this step. We then move on to landscaping, plant selection, and planting. The care of different varieties of outdoor plants, as well as houseplants, will be considered. A section follows on flower arranging and crafts.

Ideally, photographs should complement each chapter. However, instead of photographs, we have included many line drawings and recommend that you leaf through seed and nursery catalogues, usually free for the asking, for photographs of the plants mentioned.

Chapter 1
Site and Soil Preparation

Site Selection

You cannot always select a piece of property with gardening in mind but, if you can, choose land that slopes gently to the south and is sheltered from the prevailing winds to the west and north. Such a garden will receive the maximum sunshine, important for plant growth, and in the early spring and autumn will drain off cold air that causes frost damage. Shelter from the wind is important because wind damages and cools plants, thus slowing their growth. Some air movement is necessary, however, to reduce the risk of fungal infections. This is the ideal situation, but fences and hedges provide shelter, and thoughtful planning of the layout of the garden can avoid other problems such as unwanted shading and interference with power lines.

Soil Preparation

Time spent on this step is time well spent. I was told about an engineer who decided to take up gardening as a hobby and, after reading gardening books, had his lot excavated to 3 feet (1 m) and filled with topsoil. Most of us are faced with a moonscape in a new subdivision and a limp bank account. Fortunately, there are other ways besides complete excavation.

If you have no soil whatsoever (just grey subsoil and rocks), you might want to use raised beds. These, constructed of four-by-fours (10 cm by 10 cm) or concrete blocks, are simply walls to contain the soil.

They should be 12 inches (30 cm) or, preferably, 18 inches (45 cm) high and no wider than 5 feet (1.3 m) so that you can work on them from each side and reach the middle. If the beds are any higher, there will be problems with freezing right through the soil during the winter and many perennial plants and shrubs will be lost. The beds can be of any length and laid out in any pattern in the yard. Some wood preservatives damage plant roots, so care is needed when choosing wood for beds. Linseed oil (raw or boiled) protects wood from rot. Paint the oil on the wood before construction begins and then every few years, especially where the wood is in contact with the soil.

Use good topsoil to fill raised beds. What is good topsoil? It can be purchased or made. Start with soil, the browner the better. Add as much organic matter – compost, manure (be prepared for weeds), leaves, or peat – as possible. Be careful with peat as it holds water well, but when it dries it is difficult to re-wet; the addition of soapy water (dish detergent) or a small amount of phosphate will solve this problem. Do not add more than about one-quarter peat by volume; add it to the soil in the bottom of the bed, no closer than 6 inches (15 cm) from the surface of the soil. A commercial fertilizer may be needed for the first few years. Check the pH of the soil to determine if you need to add agricultural lime. If the organic matter is not well decomposed, add a fertilizer higher in nitrogen (the trio of numbers on fertilizers [e.g., 20-6-8] indicates the proportions of nitrogen-phosphorus-potassium) to feed the decomposers (microbes). Add more organic material each year.

If you have some semblance of soil, then you can prepare beds (see Chapter 2 for positioning beds). Beds refer to flower beds, vegetable beds, and shrubberies, etc. If the area is sodded, only a slight modification is needed to produce beds. Stake out the bed and get started. Remember that small is beautiful; it is better to prepare a new small bed well each year and enjoy it than to burn out in a massive effort. Remove sods by cutting 1-foot squares with a hand sod cutter, then lift out the squares with a garden fork or spade (Figure 1). Loosen the soil with a pick before digging it out. Throw the rocks into a wheelbarrow and discard. Dig a trench the width of the bed by 1 foot (30 cm) wide and as deep as possible – 8 inches (20 cm) is good but 18

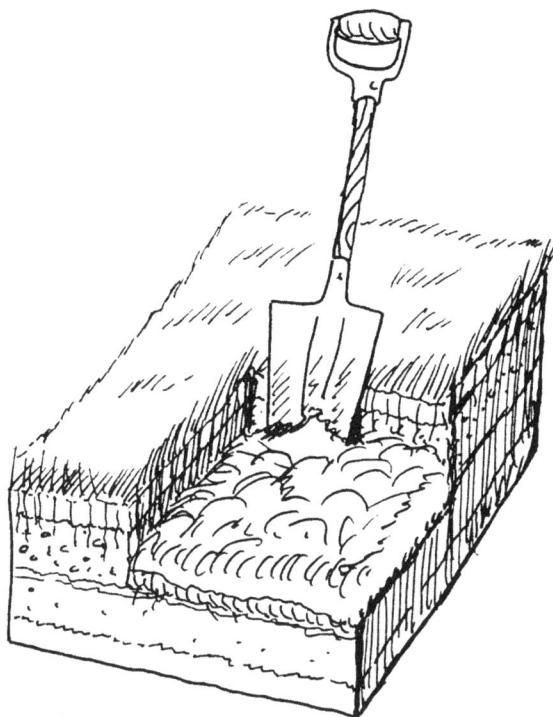

Figure 1. Bed preparation.

inches (45 cm) is better. Put the sods in the trench upside down; bury them well or they regrow. Put about 6 inches (15 cm) of peat mixed with leaves collected the previous fall into the trench before replacing the soil. Add grass clippings to the surface of the soil throughout the summer and more organic material each year. This is not easy work, so I prepare my beds by doing one trench (1 ft by 4 ft / 30 cm by 120 cm) each civil weekday afternoon before supper. It can take me the entire summer to finish a long bed, but doing it this way does not seem such a horrendous chore and weekends are then free for enjoyable chores and other pursuits. Do not plan to plant a bed the same year as you prepare it. I have taken this route and it does not work. Haste makes waste! However, as you will likely be anxious to plant, put a container by the door – a half-barrel, old bathtub, or whatever you have on hand – fill it with soil and plant it.

Lawns

Lawns require a deep layer of soil in order for them to become green carpets of the future. Many people with new homes rake a skim of soil over the rocks and lay sods (Figure 2, left). This does not work. We may have wet summers for many years when lawns grow well, followed by several dry summers that produce large yellow patches. Many homeowners then cry "cinch bug" and engage in chemical warfare. Cinch bugs, which have an odd odour, are associated with over-fertilization. In many cases, digging away the dead patch of lawn reveals a pile of rocks or some other form of excessive drainage. Grass must be able to root deeply to survive dry spells, and this requires reasonable soil all the way down. Most new city lots are a grim prospect, but they must be tackled if a good lawn is to be achieved. Caches of boulders, building material, garbage, and car wrecks must be removed or buried deeply. Rake off the large rocks and spread at least 6 inches (15 cm) of reasonable soil (Figure 2, right). Grade and roll it. Chapter 4 discusses lawns in more detail.

Proper soil preparation is critical to long-term enjoyment of a garden. There is no substitute. Start small and keep at it.

Composting

Let it rot! Organic matter is critical for healthy plant growth. It improves the texture of soil, increases its water-holding ability, and assists plants in taking up nutrients. It is an excellent soil amendment (Figure 3). Almost anything can be composted – leaves collected in the autumn, grass clippings, kitchen scraps such as peelings, eggshells, and tea bags; but no animal products such as meat, bones, dairy products, or grease. Chop up thick materials like broccoli stalks and citrus peels, as smaller pieces decompose more quickly. Avoid diseased plants or weeds with flowers or seeds. Add some finished compost to get your pile started.

The rate of decomposition is determined by the ratio of carbon to nitrogen. Think of carbon as brown stuff like leaves, and nitrogen as green stuff such as grass clippings, weeds, and the green leaves and stalks of spent crops. Carbon breaks down slowly and nitrogen accelerates it by feeding the microbes (mostly bacteria and fungi).

Leaves collected in the autumn have a high carbon content. It helps

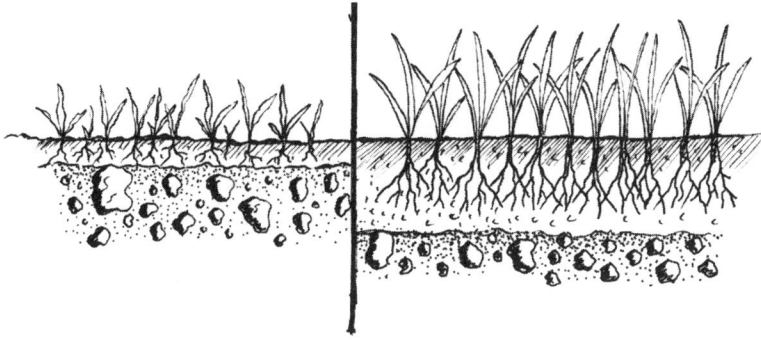

Figure 2. Lawn Preparation – Shallow layer of topsoil (left); deeper layer of topsoil (right) has lush grass.

Figure 3. Raw materials for a compost bin include leaves, grass clippings, and vegetable scraps.

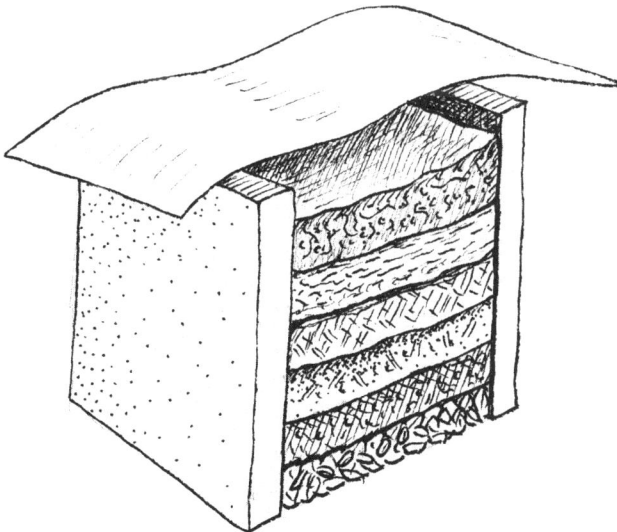

Figure 4. Compost bin with layers of materials and cover.

if you collect them with your lawn mower, as then they are chopped finely. Layer leaves with soil to speed decomposition, or store in a circular wire fence; add to your compost bin the following summer.

Compost piles should be layered – brown layer (e.g., autumn leaves), green layer (e.g., grass clippings), soil; then repeat (Figure 4). Make the piles about 3 feet by 3 feet by 3 feet (1 m³). Keep the compost ingredients evenly moist – they should feel as wet as a damp sponge. Water if necessary and in rainy weather cover with a tarpaulin. Stir the pile regularly to ensure an adequate air supply for maximum microbial action.

"Effort spent on soil preparation is effort well spent."

Notes

Chapter 2
Landscaping

Landscaping involves modifying the natural landscape with a human touch. For a new house, this is more often a matter of healing the scars and fitting into the natural landscape. Several basic principles should be kept in mind, and the rest is personal taste – it is your house and garden. Figures 5 to 8 give general ideas about what will be discussed in this chapter.

Pencil and paper is the best way to start. First, make a list of your property's assets. Is it sheltered? Does it receive much sun? Are there views you want to retain, or screen? If you have a previously owned property, you will have to work around what is there.

There are two aspects of landscaping – hardscape and softscape. Hardscape includes sidewalks, driveways, fences, raised beds, patios, garden gnomes, and other statuary, whereas softscape is the plants. To determine what landscaping features you want and their location, make a list of what you want to do on your property. Getting from the road to the door without collecting mud on your shoes is usually a priority. Parking for your vehicles is usually straightforward. If you have two vehicles, remember that there is a universal law stating that the vehicle you want is parked inside! Side-by-side parking is best. Gravel is a good foundation for a driveway and can be replaced, as finances allow, with concrete or asphalt. Paving bricks look lovely but are high maintenance as the weeds that grow between them require considerable effort to remove. Make a plot plan and sketch several routes for sidewalks. Try minimize sidewalks, but make them efficient by using them to link the driveway, entrances, and other important traffic areas. Gravel or paving blocks will do initially. Space paving blocks at least 0.5 inches (1.2 cm) apart for easy weeding. Consider snow clearing when planning driveways and walkways. Where will snow be piled? Will plantings nearby act as a snow fence and accumulate snow?

Before your plans get too advanced, consider the words I live by: Minimum effort; maximum pleasure (but I am not afraid to work).

One way to incorporate this philosophy into a landscape is to accommodate mowing of the lawn. Trimming the edges with a hedge trimmer is a waste of time and can be eliminated by having the sidewalk and driveway flush with the grass. Since grass creeps into and under pavement, a barrier is necessary. I use two-by-fours (5 cm by 10 cm) on edge or four-by-fours, painted with linseed oil, along walks, driveway, steps, and beds. The wheel of the mower can be run along the board to trim the edge neatly. Put a 6-inch-wide (15 cm) trench of gravel under fences, edged, if you like, for easy care.

The orientation of a lot will dictate where patios, trees, and beds go. In a landscaping project, the lawn is usually the next step after the driveway and walks, but, on paper, trees, shrubberies, and beds are next. The general idea is to frame the house with vegetation to help it blend in with Mother Earth, and to invite guests to your front door and then inside. Trees tie a house to the ground and frame it. The house is the focus but not a monument, so the side boundaries and rear of the property are usually planted with trees and shrubs. Trees present problems in a garden. They shade and their roots form huge mats, which make growing other plants difficult. They can also block water and sewer lines. If you want to grow predominantly flowers and vegetables, avoid large trees. There are many smaller trees available. Keep your neighbours in mind. Plant trees mainly toward the northwest of your property. If this is in front of your house, keep the trees on the periphery. The centre of the front yard should be kept free and planting done along the edges and in toward the house so that, from the street, your attention is drawn to the house and, particularly, the front door. Trees planted along the back boundary frame the house beautifully. When I look out my living room window, the bungalow across the road

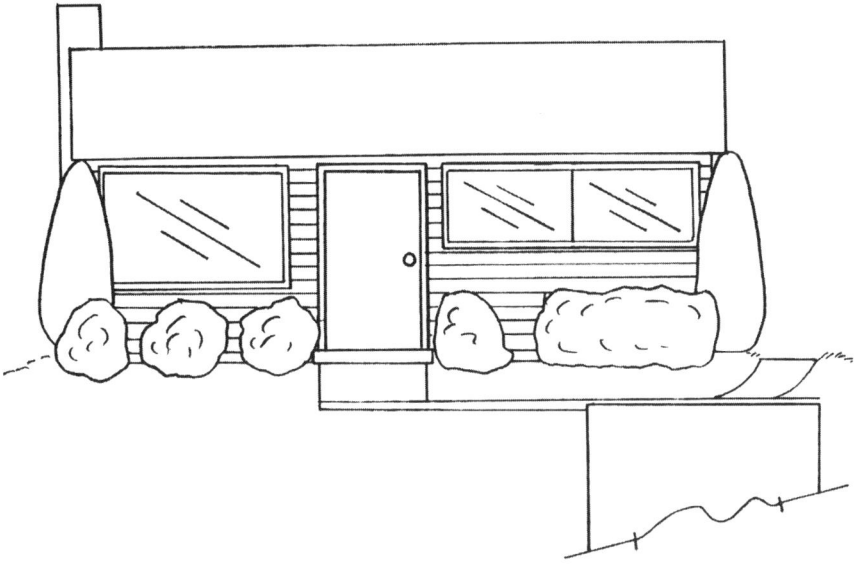

Figure 5. A bungalow with shrubs framing the entrance.

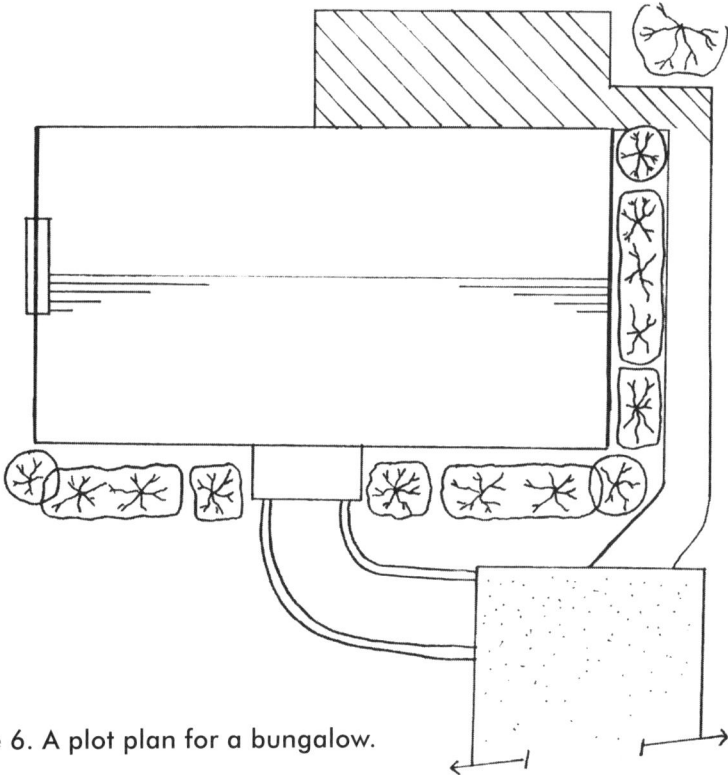

Figure 6. A plot plan for a bungalow.

has a driveway to the left, a large tree to the right, and a row of trees along the back fence. It looks so peaceful.

Shrubs can grow to 6 to 8 feet high (2-2.6 m) and are useful as frames or screens to block out undesirable views or to create privacy. Shrubs also serve as backgrounds and windbreaks for beds. Shrubs are usually planted along the front of a house and lead the eye to the front door. Some people plant rocket-shaped shrubs beside the front steps to frame the door and then sweep various shrubs across to the corners, under the windows, and place large shrubs at the corners. Others start at the corners and sweep under the windows to the doors. Spring-flowering bulbs can be planted among the shrubs, and perennials and annuals in clumps in front of the shrubs.

Some rules of thumb: rather than scatter plants, group them in odd numbers (1, 3, 5, etc.). Build up the garden gradually; you can always add more plants. Shrubbery or fences can be used as screens and windbreaks in the backyard. Patios and other features can be added as time and resources allow.

Schedule of landscaping:
1) Use a plot plan to design the layout of your yard.
2) Put in the driveway and walkways to ensure clear access to the house.
3) Establish the lawn
4) Plant trees and shrubs.
5) Prepare beds.
6) Plant beds.
7) Do the above in stages; enjoy, not dread landscaping.

Planning allows you to consider what you are trying to achieve in your yard. Changes can be made on paper more easily than in the actual yard. Layout kits (computer programs), available in some bookstores, are fun to use. Or place trees and shrubs, cut out of magazines, onto a photograph of your house to visualize your ideas if your sketching abilities are inadequate. Drive through neighbourhoods to see what you like and what you think will look good in your yard.

Figure 7. The entrance of a two-storey house.

Figure 8. The plot plan of a two-storey house.

Use your plan to keep a record of what and where you plant. This eliminates digging up a patch of bulbs or allows you to tell a curious and envious friend about which variety of gorgeous plant you have.

"When landscaping your garden, keep snow clearing and lawn mowing in mind."

Notes

Chapter 3
Weather and the Garden

A garden's environment consists of soil, rain, sun, wind, added fertilizer, and other factors. Weather is what we get day to day and climate is weather on a larger scale – the extremes and averages that the plants must cope with – the really dry or wet summer, the cold spring, etc.

The climate varies across Atlantic Canada. While it can be quite warm inland, along the coast it tends to be cooler and winters milder, with no regular spring or autumn – two seasons: cool and cooler.

The chief limiting factor for plant growth is wind. Wind cools the leaves and slows growth. A windbreak makes a big difference (Figure 9). I put a wire fence with 2-by-3-inch (5 cm by 7.5 cm) openings around my vegetable patch one year, and while I was comfortable wearing a light sweater outside the fence, it was shorts-only inside. One-inch (2.5 cm) chicken wire can be used to the windward side of a bed and is not particularly noticeable. Other types of windbreaks will be mentioned where appropriate.

The next factor important for plant growth is heat, which is associated with sunshine. In our cool climate many heat-loving plants are a struggle to grow, yet many wonderful plants elicit envy among visitors. Lupins always draw comments, and our root crops are simply the best. The growing season is short but not too short. The issue is what happens during the growing season. Warm days help growth, but cool nights set back growth. Plant varieties are often sold according to their winter hardiness, but winters are not a major problem for us (ice damage is!). Summers are, however, a problem. Many trees and shrubs do not get sufficient heat during the summer to mature their wood, and their tips die back in winter.

Rain can also be a problem for plant growth. July is often a time of drought. Even with many showery days, the ground can be powder-dry. This can be overcome by keeping the organic composition of the soil high and by adding mulch. I gradually cover all my beds with grass clippings throughout the summer, starting with the vegetables. In this way the soil is kept evenly moist, and the number of weeds is reduced and easy to pull (not including dandelions). Wait until the soil has warmed up or this layer will act as insulation and keep the soil cool.

Soil varies across the region from sand to peat. Most gardens are planted in soil formed in the last 10,000 or so years since the last glaciers retreated. It is usually fairly acidic and needs to be brought closer to a neutral pH with agricultural lime. Have your soil tested by a local Department of Agriculture representative and follow the prescribed instructions. The ideal soil pH is between 6 and 6.5 for most plants. As soil becomes more acidic or basic, the nutrients (i.e., fertilizer) become locked to soil particles and plants cannot take them up with their roots. Organic matter, like compost and peat, aids water retention and nutrient uptake, and keeps soil open to allow air to reach the roots. Sandy soils are warm because they do not hold much water, but they still need to be altered by adding organic material. In certain parts of the region, gardens must be planted in mounds because the area has only peat or peaty soil or a high water table. Mounds allow for the drainage of excess water.

Weeds

Weeds are wildflowers out of place, a curse requiring constant attention from snowmelt to snowfall. The East Coast's high precipitation gives an abundance of weeds, a curse requiring constant attention from snowmelt to snowfall. An empty 1-gallon paint tin provides a perch of the right height for me to grope and claw at these horrors. I use an old stout-bladed hunting knife for weeding. I never expect to get ahead of weeds, but I follow this basic wisdom: weed before seed is set and get all of the root. Get all of the plant out, as young as possible, before it

Figure 9. Hedges make good windbreaks (top), as do plastic (middle) and wooden (bottom) fences.

flowers. Removing all of the root is critical for dandelions, butter-and-eggs, sheep sorrel, stinging nettles, and others that can sprout from tiny fragments of underground stems (rhizomes). I expect, when I cross the river Styx, to be given a plot of ground that I must clear of sheep sorrel. I will be just downriver from the three sisters and their sieve!

Fungus

In late summer the leaves of phlox and other plants often look like they are dusted with flour. This is powdery mildew, a fungus, which can be prevented by improving ventilation around and through the plant by thinning dense stems. If the problem persists, try spraying weekly with a mixture of 1 tablespoon (15 ml) of baking soda, 1 tablespoon (15 ml) of vegetable oil, and a drop of dish detergent in 1 gallon (4 l) of water. Or, these plants can be moved to a bed with better air movement.

The environment (i.e., growing conditions) varies across the region and you are where you are. The best that you can do to optimize your garden is to reduce the effects of the wind, increase the quality of the soil, and select plants that grow well in your garden.

If a plant is not doing well despite your best efforts, compost it!

"Start small and build as you learn. Do not let your garden monopolize your spare time."

Notes

Chapter 4
Lawns

One of the first projects a new homeowner undertakes is to get a lawn growing. This is one undertaking where extra effort pays off. People have scoffed at me for emphasizing the preparation needed, with "sure, grass will grow anywhere." No question, it will. But how well? Look along roadsides and delight in all the colour and grass as you drive along. Stop and look at an area the size of your lawn. Still beautiful? Would you want that density of grass in your front yard?

A further complication has arisen lately. Many people are troubled with brown patches and moss in their lawns. The cinch bug is usually blamed, but many brown patches can be explained by thin soil, while others result from winter damage. Moss is usually said to grow in damp, shady places with poor soil, but this is not always the case. I believe we are seeing the effects of acid rain, brought with the prevailing weather systems from the central part of the continent and dumped on us. Adding agricultural lime regularly, or other recommended treatments, does not seem to cure the situation. The Japanese treasure lawns of moss, and we may have to, but unfortunately mossy lawns do not withstand much traffic.

Lawns are beautiful areas between beds where children and pets play. These areas should be properly established and cared for so that they remain an emerald carpet.

Soil preparation should be done throughout the summer. The following instructions apply to a new lawn or the rejuvenation of an old lawn (remove sods and pile them for compost; add to garden beds later). Remove the boulders on and below the surface, as well as pieces of pavement and car wrecks (which my friends found under theirs). Get rid of as many rocks as possible. Add organic material and improve the soil with agricultural lime and fertilizer. Spend time eradicating weeds: they keep germinating all summer.

The best time to lay sod or sow seeds is mid-August, as there is usually adequate moisture after this date and grass grows particularly well in cool weather. In the spring, find a tiny grass seedling. It has a few little blades, but when you dig it up you will find a good root system which developed the previous autumn.

Sods make a quick lawn, but make sure that you get high-quality sods from a nursery. I have seen coarse sods that appear to have been whipped out from under local hoofed creatures. Look for sods that have short soft leaves of grass with no weeds or stalky grass. Clover, the true culprit behind grass stains on clothing, produces a patchy appearance on lawns. Buy sods or a lawn seed mixture without clover. After you have spent many back-breaking hours preparing the soil, rake the lawn area level and leave it for a week or so to settle. Rain or a sprinkler helps this. Give the soil a good watering and then roll out the sods and cover the area with them. Use a lawn roller to make sure that the sods are in good contact with the soil; water regularly for several weeks. If seeding, level the lawn area, let it settle, sprinkle the seeds as evenly as possible, roll lightly, and water. Birds will visit newly seeded lawns but the roller pushes most seeds beyond their reach. When the grass (sod or seed) is about 1.5 inches (4 cm) tall, mow it.

Regular lawn maintenance involves liming in the spring and fertilizing in mid-August with an all-purpose fertilizer (e.g., 6-12-12). Apply lime and fertilizer on a dry day so that they do not stick to the grass blades and damage them (Figure 10). Keep children and pets off the lawn for several days. The amount of lime or fertilizer to be applied will depend on the condition of your soil – have your soil tested and follow the directions you are given or those printed on the container. Mow regularly so that grass height is about 2 inches (5 cm) high, 3 inches (7.5 cm) in the summer. It is not wise to cut the grass too short, especially during the summer when drought can be a problem. Also,

Figure 10. Use a spreader to apply lawn fertilizer.

taller grass reduces the number of weeds. I collect grass clippings for mulch.

Weeding should be done by hand as weed-killing chemicals are toxic if misused, and, with our high precipitation, I have found them especially ineffective. Deal with dandelions when they are small. Once they have matured and sent down their roots, they are the devil's own. Most people hit their lawns in spring and dig out each dandelion as it flowers. It is easy to see them then, but few of us can extract all of the root. It only takes a small fragment of root to regenerate a whole new plant. Also, a bare patch on a lawn is an ideal spot for a seed to land and germinate. Pilots have reported seeing dandelion seeds at 35,000 feet, so the plants in your lawn could be from seeds blown over from Australia! August is a better time to extract dandelions. A lawn with a good foundation of soil will not need watering. Mow the grass as late as possible in autumn so the grass is short for winter. Long grass under snowbanks can get moldy and die (the winter damage mentioned earlier).

"Use mulches in your garden."

Notes

Chapter 5
Trees and Shrubs

A lawn provides a carpet, and trees and shrubs form the foundation of landscaping. These woody plants serve as windbreaks, screens, and backgrounds, and to anchor the house visually to its surroundings. Trees and shrubs can also act as snow fences, so consider the snow clearing of driveways and sidewalks before planting them. Trees and shrubs take time to grow so they are usually planted during the first year of landscaping. The positioning of woody plants was discussed in Chapter 2; here we examine the selection of these plants.

Rule #1: do not plant maples, willows, or poplars. They form extensive root mats which take up most of the nutrients, making it difficult to grow other plants in the area of the tree; these trees can also grow through concrete walls and fill water and sewer lines with roots. Willows are messy because they continually drop leaves and branches. Poplars are short-lived, and the Trembling Aspen and Silver Maple (both are types of poplar) form large groves in no time. If you have problems growing trees and you are desperate to have trees in your landscape, then maples may be your only choice. Plant them in the northwest part of your property, away from septic systems, water and sewer lines, and power lines.

Other trees may not be good choices because of their associated pest and disease problems; for example, birch has many insect pests, cherries get Black Knot and fire blight, and pines the pine sawfly.

Remember, trees will grow. If you plant them close together to get early results, be prepared to thin the trees so that the branches of neighbouring trees do not touch. The same applies to shrubs. Do not plant them under eaves or closer than 3 feet (1 m) from a basement wall. Try to see a mature specimen. Since I am throwing out dos and don'ts, do not scatter trees and shrubs all over the lawn – clump them, preferably along the edges.

A list of trees and shrubs at the end of this chapter will help with selection. Hedge shrubs, which also fall into this section, are shrubs planted fairly close together in rows and pruned into shape. Trees and shrubs purchased from local nurseries will come in pots or with the root-ball tied up in burlap. Mail-order trees and shrubs may come in pots, with root-balls tied in burlap, or with bare-root. Check nursery trees and shrubs for injured bark (reject); and look for a pleasing shape and plump buds.

Before getting the plants, dig a hole about twice as big as the root mass and remove the rocks. It used to be recommended that this hole be filled with good soil, but research has shown that roots tend to stay in that soil and the new tree or shrub never gets well established. If the plant is bare-root, soak the roots in a pail of water overnight or at least for five to six hours before planting. Move the plant to the hole and remove it from its container. If the roots are wrapped tightly around the outside of the ball, tease them apart. Try not to disturb the roots too much and do not let them dry for even a few seconds. When roots dry, they die.

Arrange the plant in the hole and fill the soil back in, packing it around the roots so that there are no air pockets. Do not bury any of the trunk that was not buried before, as the bark will die. Then, water, water, water. For best results, water the tree or shrub regularly (once a week, even when it rains) during its first growing season. A rule of thumb is 1 gallon per foot (4 l per 30 cm) of height each week until mid-September. One thorough watering per week is much better than several small waterings as it encourages deep rooting. If the tree is 4 or more feet tall (1.3+ m), place a sturdy stake about 4 inches (10 cm) from the trunk on the windward side and tie it to the tree with a soft fabric or a short piece of water hose over rope and use a spacer to keep the tree away from the stake (Figure 11). Three guy ropes can be used

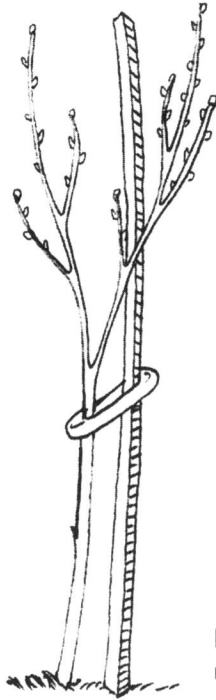

Figure 11. Staking a
newly planted tree.

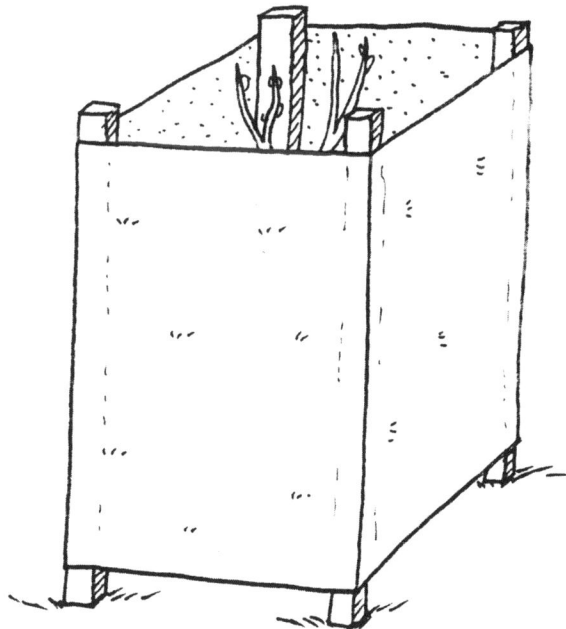

Figure 12.
Winter
protection.

for support with water hose to protect the tree from chafing. Leave the stake in place until the tree is well established and sturdy, possibly several years.

Trees and shrubs can be transplanted from the wild and some of our native species are particularly attractive. Dig the hole ahead of time; choose a small, easily dug specimen, get all possible roots (small roots are the feeding roots), wrap the roots and keep them moist; and plant as outlined above.

It is often recommended that newly planted trees and shrubs be pruned, but I usually cut off only the broken and dead bits.

Winter protection can be a problem. Heavy snow and freezing rain break branches. Evergreens can dry out in the winter and must be protected from drying winter winds. Planting the shrub where it will be sheltered in the winter is the best solution. Winter protection should prevent breakage. A framework of wood provides support (Figure 12), with burlap attached. Take care, however; too much wrapping can lead to fungal problems. I practise benign neglect in my garden and in the autumn all I do is cut down my hybrid tea roses (not the shrub roses) to about 8 inches (20 cm) and grandifloras and floribundas to 12 to 15 inches (30-38 cm) as I have lost too many stems to snow damage.

Spring is the time for pruning. Here are general guidelines that should get you through most situations. Use a sharp tool like pruning shears, a hacksaw for larger branches, and larger saws for bigger jobs. Cut the main stem or twigs just above a bud on an angle (Figure 13). Cut larger branches close to the trunk and be careful not to strip the bark. Avoid stripping the bark by first cutting from below (Figure 14). When pruning, cut dead branches first and then any branches that are crossing and rubbing. Thin out some of the branches so that light can get into the crown. A bird should be able to fly through the crown of a tree between the main branches. I cut out the biggest stems of the shrubs, right to the ground, every few years. Trim tips to achieve the desired shape. Decide who is in charge. Many people are amazed that anything grows, and they have a hard time cutting off any bits.

Fertilizer is usually not required, but, if you want to add some, it should be applied to the soil or grass under the tips of the branches,

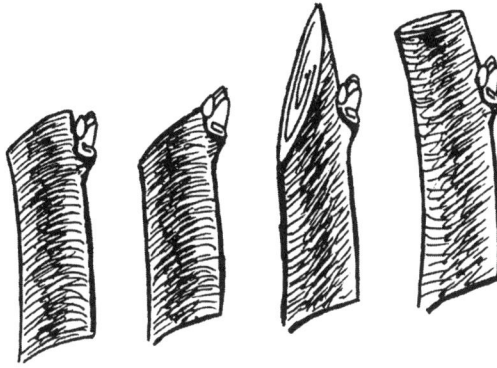

Figure 13. Pruning twigs. The one on the left is correct, as the cut is just above the bud.

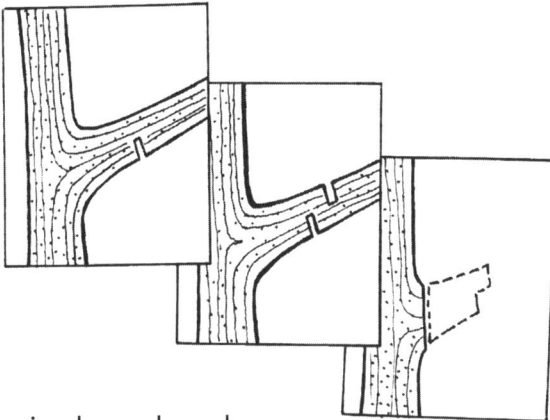

Figure 14. Pruning larger branches.

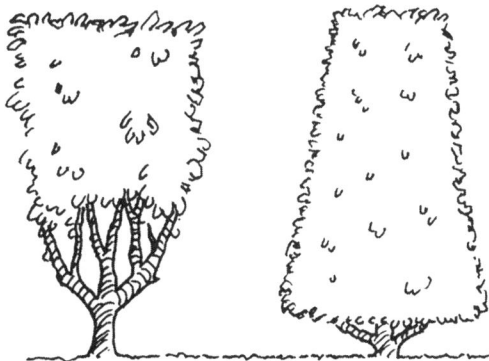

Figure 15. Pruning hedges – the one on the right is correct.

which is where the feeder roots are located. Compost can also be added. Do not apply too much fertilizer, as this encourages rampant growth, which will then be susceptible to winter injury.

Some shrubs are attacked by bugs. If the damage is not too severe then leave the bugs, as they make good food for birds. Spraying to get rid of bugs is not a good idea, environmentally, but if you do spray then use an environmentally friendly spray like the bacterium Bt or an insecticidal soap.

Many gardeners spread mulch under their shrubs to avoid weeds and to maintain even moisture. I often get to the shrubs with grass clippings after the other beds are done, but you can also use bark chips or broken bricks (available at garden centres). Gravel can be used, but you need to lay down landscape cloth (a black woven plastic material) to allow water to pass through but keep the gravel from mixing with the soil. A two-by-four, four-by-four, or brick edging around areas of shrubbery makes mowing the lawn easier and keeps a neat border.

Hedges are nice features if you have sufficient room. They are planted about 18 to 24 inches (45-60 cm) apart in a row and clipped into almost any shape, as long as it is widest at the base (Figure 15) to ensure leaves right to the ground.

The following lists include trees and shrubs that grow well with minimal fuss, as well as some, which, although they may need special treatment, are worth the effort. Their Latin and common names used in catalogues are included. This is not a definitive list, merely recommendations. If you see a plant in a catalogue that is not listed here and is recommended for hardiness zones 1, 2, or 3, it should be suitable; zone 4, probably; and zones 5 and 6, maybe, in the average garden.

Trees
- Ash (*Fraxinus excelsior*) – grows well.
- Balsam Fir (*Abies balsamea*) – can be transplanted from nature.
- Beech (*Fagus sylvatica*) – wonderful trees, spread out so give them lots of room. Two varieties are available: bronze-leafed, copper beech, and a nice weeping form in addition to the green-leafed one.

- Cherry (*Prunus*) – some sour cherries do well but, if you plant them, a warm location is needed. Sweet cherries do not do as well. Cherries are subject to Black Knot, a difficult-to-control fungus, found also on wild cherries (a source of infection). Some control Black Knot by spraying with powdered sulphur before the leaves unfold. In recent years another fungal disease, fire blight, has attacked cherries.
- Crabapple (*Malus*) – some varieties grow nicely, but others have diseases that produce unsightly leaves.
- Dogberry (*Sorbus*) – also called mountain ash and rowan tree. A nice small tree if not denuded by mountain ash sawfly.
- Goldenchain (*Laburnum watereri*) – a wonderful tree, often self-seeds, so get small trees from friends. Does not grow in many places in Canada, but does well in Newfoundland.
- Hawthorn (*Crataegus*) – not recommended because pests strip its leaves.
- Horse Chestnut (*Aesculus hippocastaneum*) – white with pink flowers. Spring winds damage young leaves.
- Larch, Tamarack, Juniper (in Newfoundland) (*Larix laricina*) – suitable for a moist site. Can be transplanted from nature.
- Lime, Linden, or Basswood (*Tilia*) – grow into lovely large trees with a wonderful perfume from their flowers in July.
- Manitoba Maple (*Acer negundo*) – does not have a typical maple leaf but grows fast. Norway Maple (*Acer platanoides*) – a large maple with all of the problems associated with maples.
- Oak (*Quercus*) – English oak (*Quercus robur*) and some oaks native to eastern Canada do well here.
- Pines (*Pinus*) – pines prefer sandy, warm soils. Attacked by pine sawfly (use Bt to kill this pest).
- Red Horse Chestnut (*Aesculus carnea*) – red-flowered, large tree. Young leaves are subject to damage by wind in spring.
- Red Maple (*Acer rubrum*) – a native tree, can be transplanted from nature or purchased from a nursery.
- Spruces (*Picea*) – spruces (e.g., Colorado blue spruce) grow well but have pest problems such as spruce budworm (use Bt to kill budworms).

- Sycamore Maple (*Acer pseudoplatanus*) – widely planted. Large tree, typical maple, but not wonderful.
- White Beam (*Sorbus aria*) – whitish, lobed leaves and a cluster of vermilion berries.
- White Birch (*Betula papyrifera*) – these beautiful trees are attacked by a number of pests and I do not recommend them. Usually do not do well if planted in the open by themselves.

Shrubs
- Amur Maple (*Acer ginnala*) – clump-forming shrub.
- Beauty Bush (*Kolkwitzia amabilis*) – gorgeous shrub; does well.
- Burning Bush (*Euonymus alatus*) – has a winged stem, fruit, a spectacular autumn colour, and is deciduous.
- Bush Honeysuckle (*Lonicera tartarica*) – not recommended. Plagued by pests.
- Cedars (*Thuja occidentalis*) – cedars prefer moist non-acidic soil.
- Chuckley Pears (*Amelanchier*) – native shrubs with lovely white flowers and good fruit, usually ruined by a rust fungus.
- Cotoneaster (*Cotoneaster*) – upright and creeping varieties. *Cotoneaster horizontalis* does well.
- Euonymus (*Euonymus*) – evergreen shrub with broad leaves. Protect from winter winds.
- False Spiraea (*Sorbaria sorbifolia*) – robust grower, forms clumps. Needs to be controlled or it becomes untidy.
- Flowering Quince (*Chaenomeles*) – needs a sheltered location but does well. Flowers are produced low on the stems, so they tend to be hidden. Plant in a raised bed.
- Golden Bell (*Forsythia intermedia*) – shiny, green leaves and yellow flowers in the spring.
- Golden Elder (*Sambucus*) – popular yellow-leafed shrub. Individual stems are short-lived and should be cut to the ground after growing for three seasons to ensure constant new growth and to prevent attack by the exotic-looking stem borer.
- Heather (*Calluna*) and Heath (*Erica*) – do well and, with a careful selection of varieties, provide blooms for much of the year.

- High-bush Cranberry (*Viburnum trilobum*) – many nurseries sell this native plant; an attractive shrub.
- Holly (*Ilex*) – its evergreen leaves need protection from winter winds. Both male and female plants are needed for berry production. Variety names, including "stallion" and "princess," announce the sex of a bush.
- Juniper (*Juniperus*) – a number of junipers are sold, but spreading varieties grow better than upright junipers, which usually suffer from winter damage.
- Lavender (*Lavandula officinalis*) – do not plant in a sheltered location as the leaves are subject to winter rotting. A well-ventilated spot is best.
- Lilacs (*Syringa vulgaris*) – many varieties of common lilacs. Also French hybrids, and others. Beautiful shrubs or small trees with wonderful flowers. Need to be pruned regularly after flowering to keep them short enough to enjoy the flowers. Slow growing, so be patient.
- Mezereon (*Daphne mezereum*) – short shrubs (18 in / 45 cm) with pink flowers early in the season, followed by bright red berries (poisonous). Seeds sprout freely around the parent plant and are the usual source of new plants.
- Mock-Orange (*Philadelphus*) – has fragrant white flowers on a 6-foot-tall shrub (2 m).
- Ninebark (*Physocarpus opulifolius*) – not particularly attractive, but it grows well.
- Oregon Grape (*Mahonia* [*Berberis*] *aquifolium*) – broad-leafed evergreen, needs winter protection.
- Pea Bush (*Caragana arborescens*) – withstands wind and does well. Yellow, pea-like flowers.
- Pee Gee Hydrangea (*Hydrangea paniculata grandiflora*) – does well, but other varieties are not always reliable. Do not prune the tips of branches in the spring as flower buds are located there.
- Red-osier Dogwood (*Cornus stolonifera*) – one variety has bright red stems in the winter, another has yellow. Some varieties have variegated leaves.

- Rhododendron and Azaleas (*Rhododendron*) – rhododendrons are evergreen (and need protection during winter); azaleas are deciduous. Both need a sheltered location. The best specimens I have seen grew on the south side of a house or other shelter, although semi-shade is usually recommended. Of course, full sun on the East Coast is seldom blistering.

- Roses (*Rosa*) – shrub roses are the most successful garden roses; large (4-5 ft / 1.5 m). Hybrid teas are the classic type, but tend to grow for years or die after one or two seasons. Try grandifloras like "Queen Elizabeth," and floribundas. Climbing roses, particularly red varieties, do well in a sheltered location. Miniature roses and the potted roses sold for Mother's Day are rugged and grow for years outdoors.

- Russian Olive (*Elaeagnus angustifolia*) – handsome shrub with narrow silvery leaves and orange berries.

- Shrubby Cinquefoil (*Potentilla fruticosa*) – short (2 ft / 60 cm), with a profusion of buttercup-like flowers all summer. Yellow, white, pink, and orange flowers.

- Snowball Bush (*Viburnum*) – an attractive shrub.

- Snowberry (*Symphoricarpos albus*) – not recommended. Plagued by pests, becomes a pest itself by sending shoots in all directions.

- Spiraeas (*Spiraea*) – all of these grow well (1-4 ft / 0.3-1.3 m tall), ranging from "Bridal Wreath" with its sprays of white flowers to pink-flowered types and sunset-leafed varieties like "Gold Flame."

- Weigela (*Weigela florida*) – a wonderful shrub with a profusion of flowers in mid-summer.

- Withrod (*Viburnum cassinoides*) – a native shrub, is attractive in all seasons. In recent years, however, it has been defoliated by an insect.

- Yews (*Taxus baccata*) – one plant that grows reasonably well in shade. Dark green evergreens; require winter protection. Also used for hedging.

Hedges

- Barberry (*Berberis thunbergi* & *B. vulgaris*) – they make dense prickly hedges and have scarlet leaves in the autumn.
- Mountain Currant (*Ribes alpinum*) – rugged hedge plant, trims nicely, and easily propagated from twigs stuck in the ground in spring.
- Privet (*Ligustrum vulgare*) – the choice for formal or informal hedges.
- Spiraeas – several varieties for informal (shaped rather than severely pruned) hedges.
- Willows (*Salix*) – if you have a windy spot, shrub willows make a good hedge. Laurel Willow (*Salix pentandra*) has shiny leaves and does well under windy conditions. Willows need regular and fairly severe pruning to look good.
- Yew (*Taxus baccata*) – pleasing formal or informal hedge.

Vines

- English Ivy (*Hedera helix*) – good ground cover or for scrambling over a stone surface. Be certain that you want it, as it glues to rock.
- Honeysuckle (*Lonicera periclymenum*) – traditional vine. Attracts bees and wasps, so do not plant over an entranceway.
- Virgin's Bower (*Clematis*) – many beautiful colours available from nurseries. The purple *Clematis jackmani* is a reliable choice.

Ground Cover

- Periwinkle (*Vinca minor*) – evergreen that grows in shady or sunny locations. Fast-growing, makes a wonderful ground cover. Can be somewhat invasive, so give it room.

"When pruning, decide who is in charge and get cutting."

Notes

Chapter 6
Beds for Planting

The term "beds" is used in this book to indicate a plot of cultivated soil where flowering plants, vegetables, or shrubs are planted. A bed can be of any shape, depending on the lot and your landscaping ideas. Beds can be square or with edges that undulate informally down the garden (Figure 16); they can be flush with the surrounding area, raised, or on the edge of a bank. Try to blend them in: a bed in the middle of a lawn is usually not a good idea because it reduces the amount of open space to be used for other purposes; it makes maintenance more difficult; and it makes the garden look cluttered. Beds should be positioned (see Chapter 2) with sunlight and shelter in mind. The size of beds can vary, but access for plant care should be considered (planks can be used). Flower beds are usually not places you thunder through regularly and compact the soil, so they can be fairly wide, up to 6 feet (2 m) if they contain only herbaceous plants, or a little wider if shrubs are used behind the plants (details in Chapters 7 and 8).

Vegetable beds are cultivated on a regular basis and should, ideally, be long and narrow so that you can reach the centre of a bed from either side. If you have a large square garden, lay down boards for walkways to avoid soil compaction.

Raised beds have become popular in recent years and for good reasons (Figure 17). They can be filled with rich, organic soil and worked on easily. They are especially suitable if your garden is on thin, rocky soil or rock. Frames for the beds can be four-by-fours, other wooden frames, or concrete blocks. The maximum height of a bed is

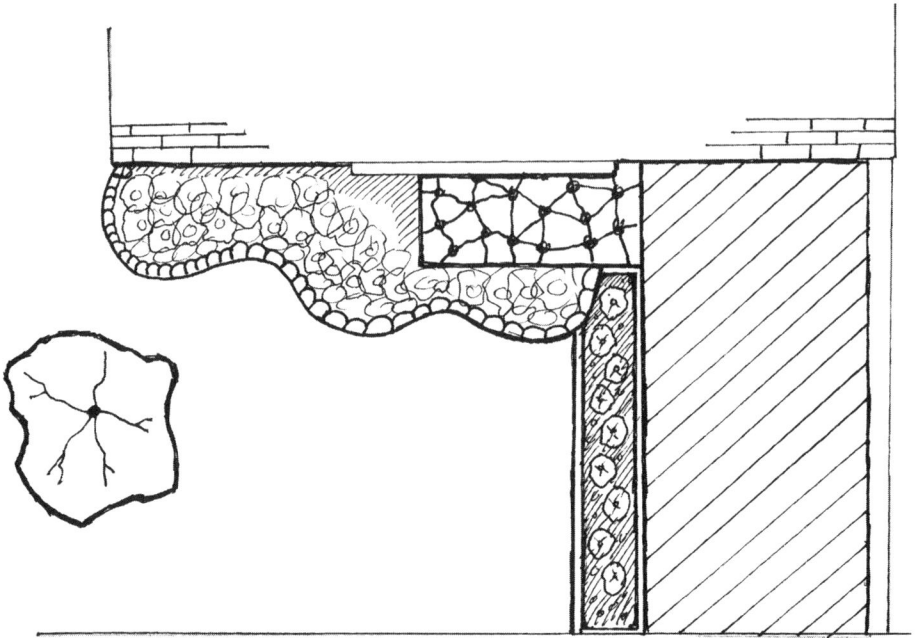

Figure 16. Beds can be informal (left) or sharply declined (right).

Figure 17. Raised vegetable bed.

Figure 18. Container gardens are ideal for balconies, patios, and decks.

about 2 feet (60 cm). Some gardeners make higher beds but experience trouble over-wintering plants in them because they freeze all the way through, and freezing and thawing damages the plants. Higher beds, which are more comfortable for gardeners with mobility difficulties, should only be planted with annuals and vegetables.

Container gardening is great for people with limited space (apartment dwellers) or used for accents on patios or steps (Figure 18). Any container – large pots, window boxes, barrels, bathtubs, car wrecks, or whatever you have on hand – can be used. Fill the container with rich, organic soil, put in the plants, make sure they do not dry out during the summer, cover it for the winter, and top dress it with compost in the spring for another season.

Beds, whether ground or container, allow the gardener to be creative. Pick a theme – colour, dried flower varieties, scent, or texture.

White gardens are classic: there are many white flowers as well as plants with whitish leaves, and the results can be exciting. A majority of flowers are yellow with a relief of blues, purples, and burgundies in the autumn when perennial asters bloom. Planning and planting can be creative and rewarding. Do not feel restricted. A scent garden near the deck, a white garden in a shady spot, a herb garden by the door near the kitchen, a vibrant kaleidoscope of colour on a sunny bank; the possibilities are endless. I have not even mentioned knot gardens or formal rose gardens.

The next three chapters will be devoted to the plants that we plunk in the ground to provide flowers in our gardening year. Annuals give a burst of colour for one year only, perennials are in for the long haul and often provide the garden's framework, and bulbs put on a show in the spring or summer. Annuals, perennials, and bulbs can be mixed or kept separate and are often combined with rocks, arbours, fences, or shrubberies. The idea is to have a succession of bloom through the growing season, which in my garden is often from late March to mid-November. The flowers are there but not always a pleasure to visit, so plant the early and late ones where they can be admired from windows.

"Wind is the chief limiting factor for plant growth on the East Coast."

Notes

Chapter 7
Annuals

Annuals are plants that grow from seed in the spring, bloom, and set seed (if they are going to) by autumn. They are noted for producing flowers of many hues and patterns. They are often planted in large patches or entire beds and are useful for planting near clumps of spring-blooming bulbs to fill in gaps after bulb leaves have died down. Many people fill a few spots in a perennial border or edge a walk or shrubbery with favourite annuals.

There are two ways to get annuals going – sow seeds (inside or out) or buy plants. I prefer to start my own plants from seeds, as certain varieties I want are often not available from nurseries. Some annuals, like petunias and snapdragons, are troublesome to get started or need to be started early; these I leave to the nursery growers. I love the perfume of petunias and plant them near a door; and few plants bloom so well and so long as snapdragons. If you prefer to start your own annuals early inside, see Chapter 12 for details. Annuals also are planted by sowing seeds directly in the garden bed.

Many seeds are best planted straight in the ground in the spring and allowed to grow with the season. These are described in seed catalogues as half-hardy annuals. In theory, seeds can be planted in the autumn, but remember where you live! Freezing and thawing and rain washes away seeds. I wait until the snow has gone and there is a civil day – usually in mid-April – and then I plant my seeds. I use a hand cultivator (Figures 19 & 20a) to loosen the soil, sprinkle a few seeds in that area (Figure 20b), and pat them in place (Figure 20c). No guessing – the seeds know when it is time to germinate. This is a useful method when you want a few annuals here and there, to cover bulbs, or to fill in between perennials or around shrubs. It can also be used for whole beds. As there are usually enough seeds in a package to plant a vast area, you will probably have reserve seeds in case of a calamity. I make a circle of small rocks around where the seeds are sown to remind me.

If you have small plants to put in the garden, make sure that they are hardened off, that is, they have been put outside in their containers for a while each day for a week or so and then gradually left outside day and night for a week before planting. They should be protected from wind and full sunlight at first or they will scorch and turn beige and/ or red. Nurseries usually harden off their plants; these plants are found outside in cold frames. You can use a cardboard box as a short-term cold frame. Plants started in the house will have to be hardened off. When plants are ready to be planted outside, dig a hole big enough for the roots and put the small plant in it. If they have been grown in flats (Figure 21), remove all the plants and cut the root mass into cubes with a plant in the centre of each cube (Figure 22). Water the newly planted seedlings well. When should you plant the seedlings in the garden? Good question. After the danger of frost and snow has passed, usually in mid-to-late June. Some people watch for lilac buds and, as they start to produce new leaves, it is time to plant seedlings.

Annuals are wonderful, as they are quick, easy, and provide masses of colour for much of the growing season. For many people, annuals evoke strong memories. There are probably no annuals that cannot be grown in our area with a little care, but the following is a list of the most successful varieties. Annuals come in packages of single or mixed colours. Nurture the smaller seedlings from a mixed package, as they are often the more unusual colours. I usually order mixed colours as I love surprises and hope to get one of the unusual hues shown in the catalogue photograph.

Drool through a gardening catalogue and consider the following varieties. I list them by height so that you can arrange them from the front to the back of the bed to have all of them visible. Use accent plants for visual effect or for scent. Plant an impressive plant like Love-

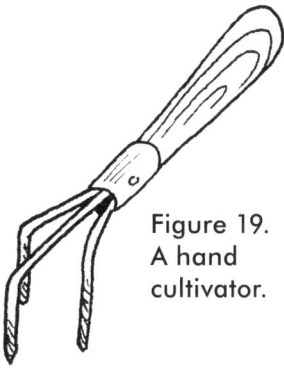

Figure 19.
A hand
cultivator.

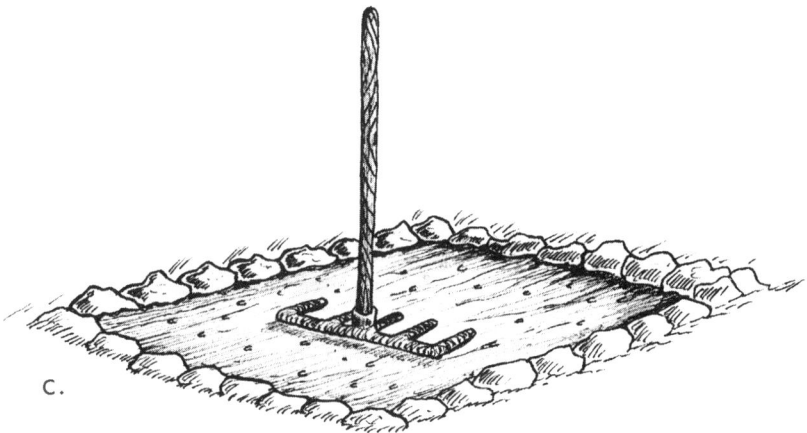

a.

b.

c.

Figure 20. Sowing seeds – a: loosen soil with a cultivator, b: sprinkle seeds, c: tamp soil with a rake.

Lies-Bleeding near the front of a bed or a clump of Nicotianas close enough to bend over at dusk for a heady sniff. Check the package or catalogue description for height, as each type of annual often comes in various heights.

Tall Varieties – back of beds or as accents (2+ ft / 60+ cm)

- Celosia – good informal effect.
- Cosmos – ferny foliage and great flowers.
- Lavatera – do well; I have seen a good show on the northwest side of a house, so they can be planted in various locations.
- Love-Lies-Bleeding – dramatic. Pick flower ropes when they first colour and dry for arrangements.
- Sweet Peas – the classic perfume flower of the garden; these need a fence or trellis to climb.

Medium Varieties – halfway back in beds or the back of narrow beds (1-2 ft / 30-60 cm)

- Balsam (*Impatiens balsamea*) – related to the patience plant.
- Butterfly Flower (*Schizanthus*) – grown as a houseplant in the cooler houses of our grandparents, who called it Spanish Shawl. Wonderfully coloured flowers. May want to start inside.
- Calendula – great autumn colour.
- Celosia or Cockscomb – exotic-looking; start inside.
- Cornflower or Bachelor's Buttons – old favourite, but try some of the new varieties.
- Dusty Miller – accent plants.
- Flowering Flax (*Linum*) – dainty flowers over a long period.
- Godetia – reminiscent of an azalea.
- Geranium (*Pelargonium*) – a perennial and a houseplant, but often grown as an annual. Forms flower buds during summer and when potted and placed in a sunny basement window will bloom through winter. Root cuttings for summer planting in February (see Chapter 12).
- Impatiens – good bedding plant that does well in shade.

Figure 21. A flat of seedlings.

Figure 22. Separating seedlings for planting.

- Kale, Flowering and Flowering Cabbage – colourful, but usually infested with cabbage larvae.
- Nicotiana or Flowering Tobacco – abundant perfume at dusk.
- Strawflower – grow for everlasting flowers to put in winter bouquets.
- Toadflax (*Linaria*) – like small snapdragons, in a variety of colours.
- Salpiglossis – velvety trumpets with golden veining. Try these.

Short Varieties – front of beds and edgings (up to 1 ft / 30 cm)

- Ageratum – great edgings. Usually started indoors.
- Asters – many varieties, but dwarf do best.
- Baby Blue Eyes (*Nemophila*) – try this one.
- Begonia, Everblooming – good plant. Keep one in the house and start taking cuttings in early March.
- California Poppy – I planted seeds of this plain orange poppy in a sunny location and it reseeds every year and provides wonderful colour for months. Pull out unwanted seedlings (note their carrot-like root). Other colours are available.
- Candytuft – plant a mass of this for a mass of colour.
- Fried Egg Flower (*Limnanthes douglasii*) – try this in a sunny location.
- Lobelia – good edging plant. Usually started inside.
- Marigolds – many sizes and varieties.
- Mesembryanthemum – a succulent plant, does well in full sun and produces daisy-like flowers, often in shocking colours.
- Nasturtium – grows best if not planted in rich soil.
- Nemesia – beautiful flowers. Better started inside.
- Petunias – best bought from a nursery. Wonderful perfume, so plant near a door or patio. Blossoms often battered by rain.
- Phlox – annual varieties form small plants with nice flowers. I like "Twinkle."
- Pinks, Annual – form good short plants.
- Poppy, Annual – scatter these around.

- Portulaca – wonderful satin-like flowers. Needs full sun.
- Salvia – popular bedding plant. Better started inside.
- Snapdragon – many varieties. Blooms until late autumn and often still growing under snow in the spring, and then killed by frost.
- Stocks – lovely perfume in early evening.
- Sweet Alyssum – sweet perfume. Great edging.
- Zinnias – good for blazing sun locations. Many varieties.

Hardy annuals which can be sown directly in the garden in late April / early May

Bells of Ireland	Calendula
California Poppy	Cornflower
Cotula	Cynoglossum
Larkspur	Lobelia
Nemophila	Nierembergia
Pansy	Scabiosa
Shirley Poppy	Snapdragon
Stocks	Sweet Alyssum

Good varieties for the beginner gardener

Calendula	California Poppy
Candytuft	Cornflower
Cosmos	Marigolds
Nasturtium	Phlox (Annual)
Shirley Poppy	Strawflower

"When watering, do not torment the plants with random sprinkles that encourage shallow rooting. Give a good deep watering less frequently."

Notes

Chapter 8
Perennials

Most people want the majority of their flowers in place and taking care of themselves year after year; perennials fit this bill. Perennials require some maintenance, but it is not continuous or critical (except for weeding).

A well-prepared bed is essential for success, and future displays of blooms can be related to the effort expended at the beginning. Perennials can be started from seeds planted straight in the ground or started inside (Chapter 12). Some bloom the first year, but most start their annual flowering the next year. The same applies to biennials, which are planted one spring and enjoyed at the appropriate time during the next growing season, after which they produce seeds and die. Perennials can also be planted as divisions of plants obtained from friends or purchased from a nursery (Figure 23). When you get a division of a plant, check its root-ball carefully to make sure you are not also getting a root of a difficult weed like gout weed or bindweed. If catalogue plants seem especially inexpensive (i.e., a too-good-to-be-true price), then caveat emptor – buyer beware. All named varieties must come from divisions as they will not come true (to variety) from seed.

Perennials are best arranged in beds from short to tall, front to back, with accent plants here and there (Figure 24). Unlike annuals, you must also consider colours and when perennials bloom so that you have blooms during the entire growing season and throughout the beds. Most perennial beds should have a fence, shrubbery, or windbreak

Figure 23. Planting a perennial.

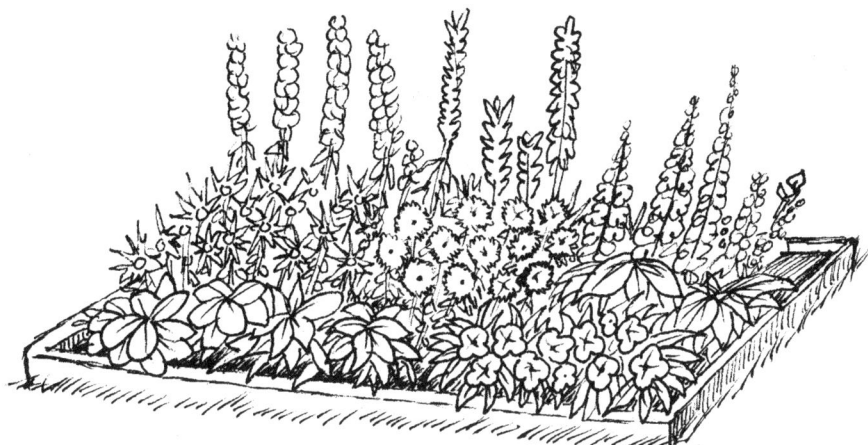

Figure 24. Plant tall perennials behind shorter ones to enhance the display of colour in your garden.

behind them. Planning ahead is necessary, as planting a perennial border is more permanent than a border of annuals. Maintenance involves staking tall plants and those, like peonies, with heavy flowers. Use twigs and branches (alders are particularly good) for staking as they "disappear" amongst the plants.

Deadhead (removing the faded flowers) regularly so that seedpods do not form. Seed production takes energy from the plant and leads to waifs all over the place. Seeds should be allowed to form on short-lived plants like pansies or biennials, which need to be reseeded. Many books recommend that perennials be cut to the ground in the autumn, but I leave old stalks to collect snow in the winter and cut them down in the spring before growth starts. This is generally recommended in recent literature. There are always glorious days in April or May when it is nice to have something productive to do.

Divide perennials every three or four years or when they need it (when the clump is large and crowded). Use a garden fork to dig up the clump (Figure 25), separate divisions with five or six stems or shoots (use a spade to slice up the clump), and replant one or two divisions. The rest can be given to friends – in this manner a garden becomes a sea of memories, with each plant reminding you of specific friends, days, and events. Spread compost or well-rotted manure around the plants in the spring; I also cover the ground between the plants with grass clippings during the summer for moisture and weed control.

Many available perennials do well on the East Coast, while others grow with some degree of fussing. My philosophy is that life is too short to surround oneself with unhappy and miserable plants – compost them. The following list includes perennials which usually do well and can form the foundation of a pleasing perennial border. Of course, there are always spaces to try out new plants. To make space, pass on some of the more obliging plants to friends.

The varieties below are listed by height, but check catalogue descriptions for height and colour as there is considerable variation within any one type of perennial. I am also going to be foolhardy enough to indicate flowering times. Remember that these times could vary by several months depending upon the year's weather. These are recommendations only, and the list is by no means complete.

Tall Varieties (2+ ft / 60+ cm) – plant at back or as accents

- Asters (*Aster*) – wonderful deep, rich colours in autumn. September.
- Bergamot or Bee Balm (*Monarda*) – enthusiastic growers. Leaves used as flavouring for Earl Grey tea. July.
- Canterbury Bells – biennial, produces masses of flowers in blue, pink, and white in mid-summer.
- Cornflower (*Centaurea montana*) – a perennial relative of Bachelor's Button. Can become a large plant; tends to sprawl, so needs to be staked. July.
- Delphinium – towering spires in blues and white. July.
- Foxglove (*Digitalis purpurea*) – make room for these. Source of the heart drug, digitalis. Biennial. July.
- Lupins (*Lupinus* Russell Hybrids) – love our maritime climate. Self-seeds. July.
- Maltese Cross (*Lychnis chalcedonica*) – an old favourite. June.
- Musk Mallow (*Malva moschata*) – an old favourite. August.

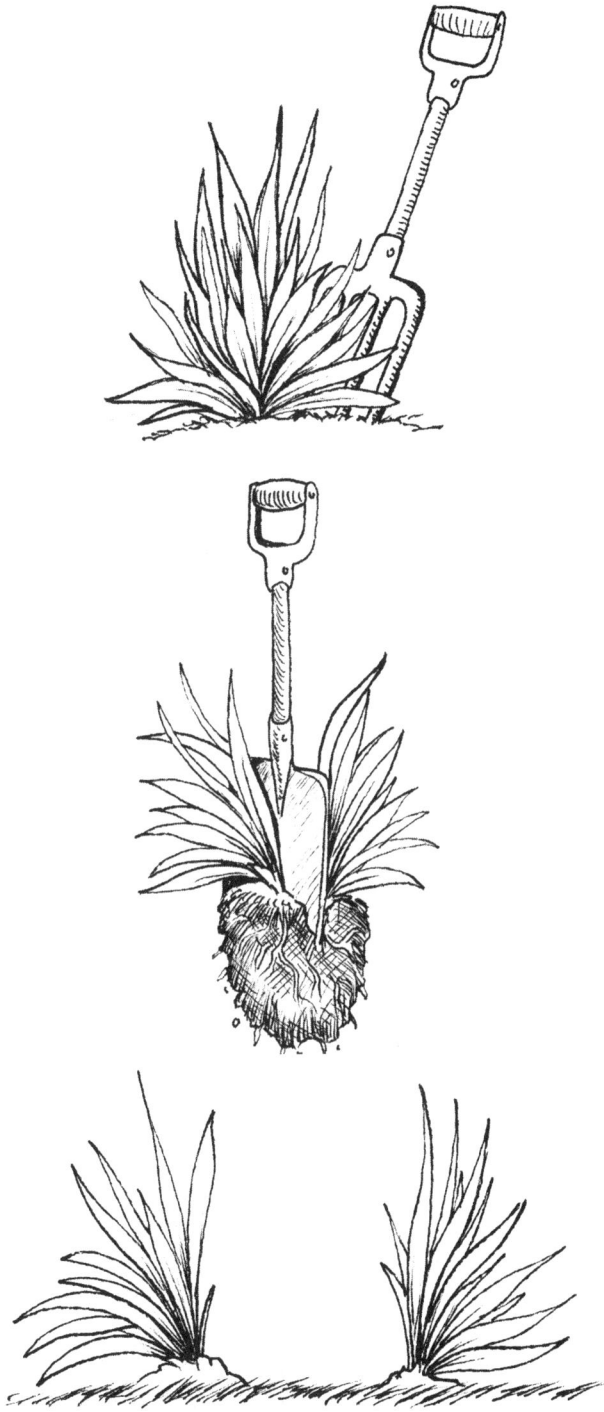

Figure 25. Dividing a perennial.

- Phlox (*Phlox paniculata*) – bright colours and fragrant. Do not allow overcrowding; give them plenty of ventilation as they are subject to unsightly powdery mildew (whitish dust on leaves) (see Chapter 3). August-September.
- Silver Dollar (*Lunaria*) – sow seeds one spring and harvest "money" the next autumn; a biennial. June.

Medium Varieties (1-2 ft / 30-60 cm)

- Asters, Midsummer (*Erigeron*) – stunning colours, daisy-like flowers. July.
- Blanket Flower (*Gaillardia*) – coarse-looking but bright flowers. August.
- Bleeding Heart (*Dicentra*) – a must. Usually a plant connected with memories. Foliage fades by mid-summer, so plant behind other plants. June.
- Columbine (*Aquilegia*) – delightful. Self-seeds. July.
- Coral Bells (*Heuchera sanguinea*) – shades of red. July.
- Flax (*Linum perenne*) – a dainty plant that blooms for much of the summer.
- Feverfew (*Chrysanthemum parthenium*) – white button flowers. Extract used in migraine remedies. August.
- Forget-me-not (*Myosotis*) – an old favourite. After flowering, looks ugly. Plant in a corner. June.
- Geum – several varieties available. July.
- Globeflower (*Trollius*) – good spring-bloomer. June.
- Lamb's Ear (*Stachys lanata*) – a plant for lovers of soft, furry things. July.
- Lily (*Lilium*) – grown from bulbs, usually planted in autumn. Asiatic hybrids are best; *Lilium regale* grows well and produces perfume at dusk; tiger lilies do well; other trumpet hybrids and oriental hybrids do not always do well in coastal gardens. July-August.
- Pinks (*Dianthus plumarius*) – with their fragrance and masses of blooms, these need a spot in your garden. Maiden Pinks do better than carnations. July.
- Poppies – Iceland Poppies grow very well. Oriental Poppies are

difficult to get established, then difficult to get rid of, but are glorious. July.

- Shasta Daisy (*Chrysanthemum maximum*) – single and double varieties; the singles look like large Ox-eye Daisies. July-August.
- Speedwells (*Veronica*) – many types; all nice. Mostly June-July.
- Sweet William (*Dianthus barbatus*) – biennial; a must for lovers of patterned flowers. July.
- Wallflower (*Cheiranthus*) – biennial; should be more widely grown. June.
- Yarrow (*Achillea*) – originated from wild yarrow. Many new colours. July-August.

Short Varieties (1 ft / 30 cm) – plant in front of bed and rock gardens

- Alyssum – Gold Dust, Mound of Gold, etc. – good spring bloom; self-seeds. June.
- Aubrietia – also called False Rock Cress. Bright colours. Either lives forever or dies over winter. June.
- Bellflower (*Campanula*) – many types of bluebells in various heights; usually do well. July.
- Candytuft (*Iberis sempervirens*) – produces a white carpet; self-seeds. June.
- Cranesbill (*Geranium*) – scented leaves. Several varieties available; some are rampant growers. July.
- Dutchman's Breeches (*Dicentra eximia*) – ferny foliage. Blooms all summer.
- Hens and Chicks (*Sempervivum tectorum*) – rock garden plant. Pink blooms on some hens in August.
- Lady's Mantle (*Alchemilla*) – not spectacular, but grows, usually enthusiastically, in shade. June.
- Pansy (*Viola*) – pansies, Johnny-Jump-Up, and violas make shows of colour; self-seeds. June onwards.
- Primrose (*Primula*) – many varieties do well. Needs some protection from full summer sun; achieved by planting next to a larger plant that towers over them later in the season. May-June.

- Rock Cress (*Arabis alpina*) – good grower. May.
- Snow-in-Summer (*Cerastium tomentosum*) – a blessing for covering a difficult area or bank, or a curse almost anywhere else; a rampant grower. July.
- Soapwort (*Saponaria ocymoides*) – good for rock gardens, banks, or front of borders. July.
- Stonecrop (*Sedum*) – good rock garden plants. July-August.
- Thyme, Creeping (*Thymus serpyllum*) – good for carpeting areas, hanging over walls, or between paving stones, as the crushed plants exude a lovely fragrance. July.
- Windflower (*Anemone*) – some grow well and multiply. Worth a try. June.

Plants for Shade

Crocus	Hosta
Periwinkle	Scilla
Solomon's Seal	Yew (*Taxus*)

"If you get insect pests in your garden, it usually indicates a basic plant health problem."

Notes

Chapter 9
Spring and Summer Bulbs

My spring starts with the first flowers of the year, usually some Winter Aconites or Snow Crocus, during the last week of March, followed by a succession of other spring-flowering bulbs. These are cheery and tough, considering their exposure to harsh weather like snow and rain.

Spring-flowering bulbs do not require special soil conditions and can be planted with other flowers or amongst shrubs in a shrubbery. For success, the basic requirements of these bulbs need to be understood. Plant bulbs as early as possible in the autumn at a depth of about two to three times their diameter, with the root side down (Figure 26). It is easy to tell up from down with tulips and daffodils because they taper upwards. With others, look for the side with a disk and a few thread-like roots or the dots where the roots have fallen off. If you simply cannot tell, plant them and the bulbs will straighten up themselves. Plant taller ones like tulips and daffodils near the back of a perennial border so that they will come up, bloom, and die down before the perennials are up. Others can be planted among shrubs. If you have spaces in the border, plant annuals or perennials by the bulbs so that the space is filled after the bulbs die down.

After bulbs are planted in the autumn, they root and lie dormant until spring. Sometimes they send up a few leaves in autumn or winter, but this is not a problem. I do not cover my bulbs with boughs for winter. In spring the flowers are produced and then the leaves. The leaves restock the bulb with stored food, and the flower bud for the next year is formed. The bulbs can be fertilized as the flowers fade. Let the leaves die down naturally.

Basic Spring Bulbs

- Autumn Crocus (*Colchicum*) – produces large broad leaves in spring and mauve flowers in early autumn.
- Allium – Flowering Onions – planted in autumn but most do not bloom until summer. Purples, pinks, whites, and yellows. Nice blooms.
- Anemone (*Anemone blanda*) – comes in a mixture of colours.
- Checkerboard Lily (*Fritillaria meleagris*) – colours are not great but checkerboard-patterned petals are interesting.
- Daffodils and Jonquils (*Narcissus*) – what is spring without these beauties? Plant in masses. King Alfred is the classic trumpet-type, but try a mixture of others (short-cup, poetaz, etc.).
- Dutch Iris (*Iris reticulata*) – this iris has pert, cheery blooms in blues, white, purples, and yellows in early spring.
- Giant Crocus or Hybrid Crocus (*Crocus vernus*) – classic crocus, larger and blooms later than Snow Crocus.
- Glory of the Snow (*Chionodoxa*) – beautiful blue flowers. Does not grow well in every garden.
- Grape-Hyacinths (*Muscari*) – lovely.
- Hyacinth (*Hyacinthus orientalis*) – fragrance and colour are wonderful. Plant near the front door.
- Indian Hyacinth (*Camassia esculenta*) – native North American plants. Blue flowers; fairly tall.
- Lilies – plant in autumn for summer bloom (see Chapter 8).
- Siberian Squill (*Scilla*) – good bulbs, grow almost anywhere in a garden.
- Snow Crocus (*Crocus chrysanthus*) – early crocus, produces masses of flowers. Highly recommended.
- Snowdrops (*Galanthus*) – one of the first bulbs to bloom in the spring.
- Striped Squill (*Puschkinia libanotica*) – small, pale blue blooms.

Figure 26. Plant bulbs at correct depths.

- Tulips – Cottage, Darwin, and Fosteriana Hybrids (like Red Emperor) do well. Most tulips gradually disappear over the years. In nature, tulips get baked in the soil over the summer; however, I suspect that the soil in this region is largely too cool and moist. My neighbours have had a spectacular display for many years. Their bulbs are planted by a rock wall and stay dry and warm over the summer. I have planted on top of a rock wall and this also works.
- Winter Aconite (*Eranthis hyemalis*) – small plants with big buttercup-like flowers, bloom as snow melts.

Summer-Flowering Bulbs

Summer-flowering bulbs (mostly tubers, corms, etc.) can be mixed with other plantings, but many gardeners prefer to have special beds for them. Prepare the beds as usual and add compost each year. Even moisture in the soil throughout the summer is easily achieved with a layer of mulch.

Over-wintering is done in a cool place (10°C). In autumn wait for the plant to die down or get hit by a frost. I record the date my dahlias turn black with frost as the first killing frost. I dig them up about a week later, but other bulbs could be dug sooner. Spread bulbs on newspapers to dry for about a week. I cut down my dahlias as I dig them (tip: tie tags to the stalks before frost or identification will be impossible), but wait for others, like gladioli, to dry. With most, remove old stems. For gladioli, cut stems just above the corm (1 in / 2.5 cm). Begonia and calla bulbs can be packed in dry peat in a box (Figure 27), while gladiola and dahlia bulbs should be wrapped in newspapers (Figure 28). Experiment to see what works best under your conditions. Avoid using plastic as it usually leads to rot. Store in a moist (not dry, but not dripping wet), dark (to discourage early sprouting), and cool (ideally 5-10°C; most basements have a corner at this temperature) place. A root cellar for storing bulbs and vegetables and forcing bulbs is the dream of most gardeners, but few have one. I place my newspaper-wrapped dahlias in a box and set it in a cool corner. This works well.

Common Summer-Flowering Bulbs

- Acidanthera – a relative of the gladiolus; pretty and fragrant. Give it a warm, sheltered location.
- Anemone – Windflower – lovely flowers; varieties such as "The Bride" are widely available. Soak corm overnight before planting and mix a little lime in the soil. Some varieties over-winter, but others need to be stored during winter. Usually sold in spring.
- Begonias, Tuberous – several flower shapes; upright and hanging basket varieties. Upright plants often have huge, wonderfully coloured flowers. Can be started inside, then planted outside when you put out seedlings. Magnificent specimens are best grown in large (about 10 in / 25 cm) pots and set outside in sheltered locations. Catalogues recommend planting in shade, but on the East Coast full sun is often equivalent to partial shade elsewhere. Does best when given sun until late morning.
- Caladium – look lovely in catalogues, but require constant heat. Best grown inside.
- Calla – grows outside, but does better in a sunporch.
- Dahlia – I am fond of dahlias. Available in a wide range of colours, forms, and sizes – from dinner plates to pompoms. Should be grown as above. In spring, divide the mass of tubers so that each clump you plant has four to five tubers. Make sure that part of the old stem is still attached, as that is where the sprouts arise. Plant in early June, with the top of tuber about 2 inches (5 cm) below soil

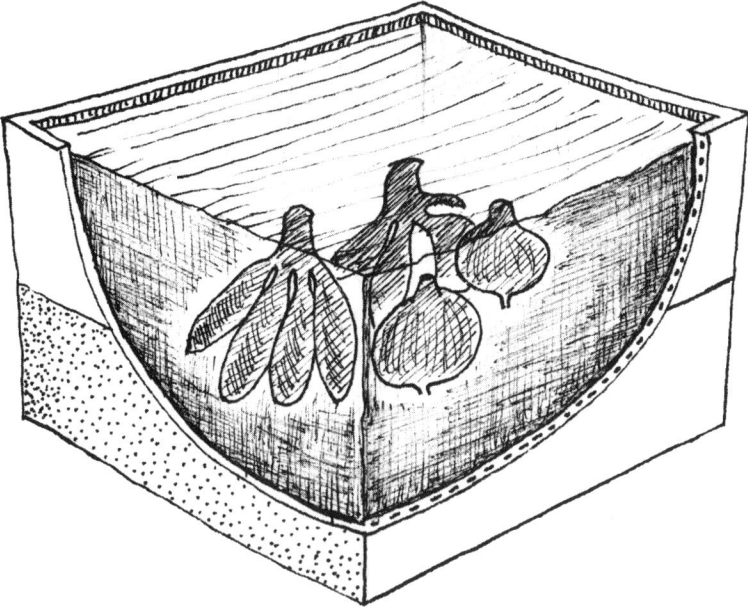

Figure 27. Storing gladioli and dahlias in dry peat.

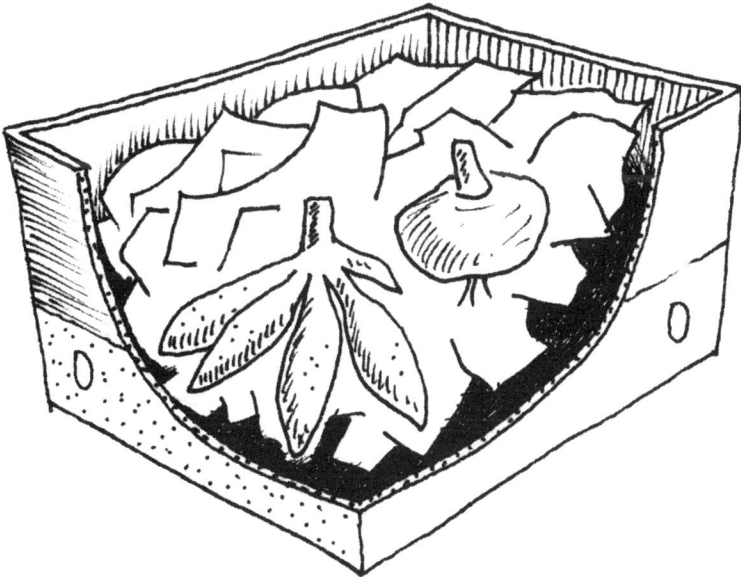

Figure 28. Gladioli and dahlias can be stored in newspaper.

surface. Do not fill in the hole but leave a depression to collect heat. Fill in as stems grow.

- Gladiolus – bold statements are made with glads. They do better in a warm, sunny, not windy location. Carefully clean off old papery coverings before planting. Plant in a hole about 6 inches (15 cm) deep and gradually fill in as the plant grows. Standard glads come in many beautiful colours. Miniatures do well and are pretty.
- Montbretias – lovely flowers. Usually over-winter if planted in a warm location such as the south side of a house.
- Ranunculus – Persian Buttercups – worth a try.
- Tigridia – Mexican Shell Flower – few people grow these, but those who do call their friends to come and look: they are spectacular. Prefer heat.

"Buy a hardcover record book and note the varieties bought, where you planted them, how they grew, etc. This is one of the best things you will ever do in your gardening life."

Notes

Chapter 10
Vegetables

Considerable satisfaction can be derived from a short harvesting trip to the vegetable patch. Fresh vegetables are the ultimate for nutrition and taste. They also give the grower a certain feeling of affluence, if ever one was to fill out a balance sheet.

Preparation of the bed is essential. Little flaws or inadequacies can be overlooked in the perennial border, but are unappealing on a dinner plate. The bed should be deeply dug. Experiment to find the right balance between mineral soil and organic material (peat and compost). The soil may be too rich, resulting in many leaves but poor roots. That may be great for Swiss Chard, but not for tomatoes. Build gradually and when you get good results add back enough organic material each year to maintain that level. Supplement with a chemical fertilizer – an all-purpose fertilizer is suitable – if you wish. Check the pH of the soil and add agricultural lime to bring it up to pH 6 (apply 10 lb per 100 ft^2 initially, and then 5 lb per 100 ft^2 each year). Soil pH is important because if the soil is too acidic or too alkaline the nutrients become locked to the soil particles. Organic material is important not only for moisture retention and to give the soil an open texture but also to aid the plants in taking up nutrients. Particles of organic matter act as intermediaries between soil grains, where nutrients are often found, and root hairs, where nutrients are absorbed by the plants.

A vegetable patch functions best when all of the crops are harvested each fall or by early spring. Plant rhubarb and other perennial crops off by themselves. Many manuals recommend that you dig the vegetable bed in the autumn. This is best, but it is often too wet in the autumn and/or there are still plants in the ground until November and it is not practical. I wait for one of those glorious days in April when the ground is fairly dry and the day is wonderful. Add compost and dig the bed. Extensive digging is probably not necessary, but you feel good afterwards. Arrange your beds so that you can walk about them without compacting the soil. Raised beds (see Chapter 6) or edged beds work well (Figure 29). A concept we studied in early English history at school was the rotation of crops; this is still a good idea. Each type of plant uses different amounts of nutrients for its growth, so if you grow the same type of plant year after year in the same soil it will use up its required nutrients. Each year draw up a planting plan during the winter and keep it from year to year. This will help with rotating crops and with keeping track of the varieties you have tried. Location of the bed is important. Vegetables require full sun all day and protection from wind, but some air circulation is necessary. Check your property; locate your vegetable garden where the snow is deepest, provided it is sunny, as this is the most sheltered spot.

Many varieties of vegetables can be grown on the East Coast; root crops, in particular, excel because of our cool summers. After you decide upon a slate of vegetables, select types and varieties. For example, there are Nantes, Touchon, and Chantenay carrots and then varieties of each of these. Each year I order my old reliables and one or two different varieties. Those that do well for me may not for you, and vice versa. Ask other growers in your area what they are growing, and why. Sometimes people like the harvest or the flavour, etc. An advantage of growing several varieties is that in our unpredictable weather one variety should grow no matter what the conditions happen to be.

What to do with all the seeds, you might ask. Most packages have enough seeds to plant an entire garden, so there are always many left over. Order seeds with friends, and share; store seeds in a jar or plastic bag in the refrigerator between plantings. Most seeds remain viable for several years, many years in the case of tomatoes. Others, like parsnip, do not keep.

Planting is fairly straightforward. Rake the surface of the bed so that the soil is fine and lump-free. This ensures good contact with the seeds

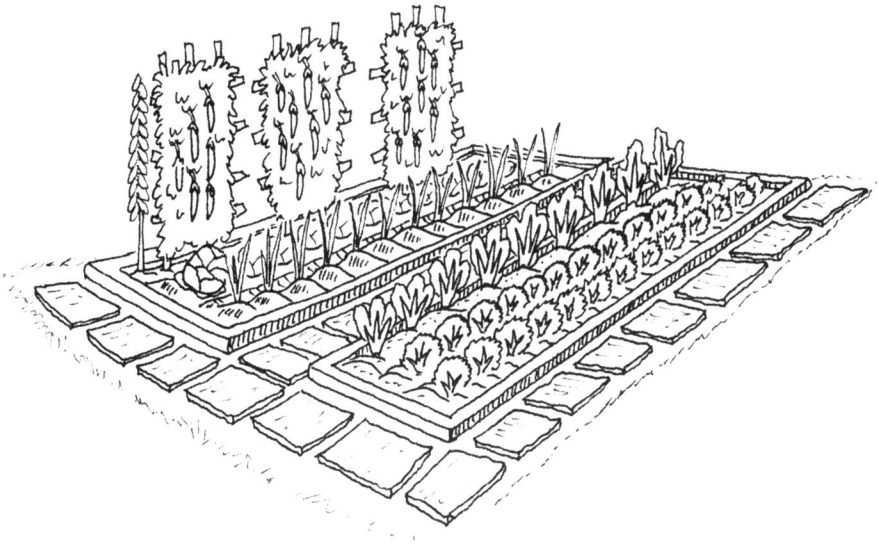

Figure 29. Vegetable garden with raised beds and walkways.

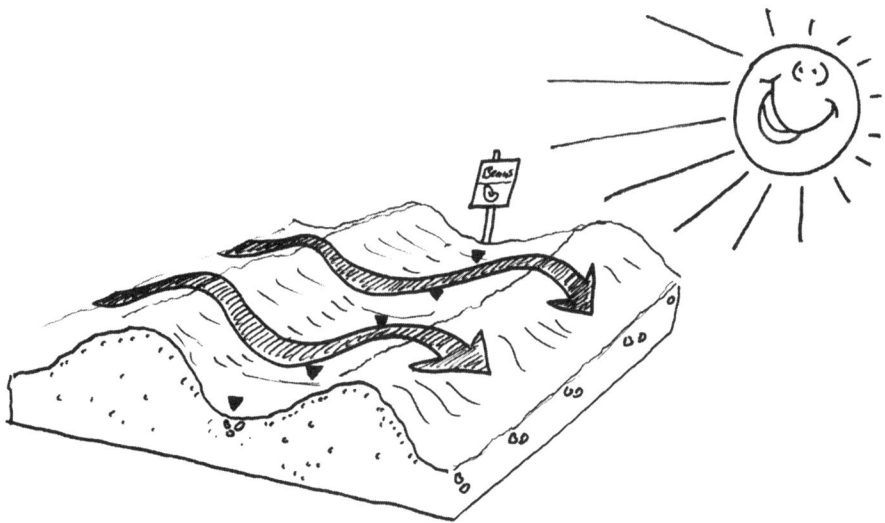

Figure 30. Seeds planted in trenches.

and they achieve better germination. Some seeds can be planted in areas, others in rows. To decide on the best layout, consider the growth form of the plant, its size when mature (width for spacing and height for shading), the weeding, and the cultivating. I plant many vegetables in rows. My garden slopes to the south and I dig furrows with an east-west orientation. Using a hoe, I pull the soil to the south, leaving the trench with a steep cliff to the north and a slope to the south. This allows the sun to warm the soil and the wind to blow over it (Figure 30). The little heat we get must be maximized. Trenches are also fairly deep (about 4 in / 10 cm) with seeds planted at the correct depth in the bottom of the trench and then filled in as the plants grow.

Seeds are planted three to five times their diameter below the soil surface. This works out to 0.5 inches (1.3 cm) for small seeds and 1.5 to 2 inches (4-5.3 cm) for larger seeds like beans and peas. Since seeds are inexpensive and plentiful, it is best to plant early and often. Most people plant their seeds too late and lose valuable growing time. Beans, however, are usually planted too early. Beans, corn, cucumber, and zucchini must have warm soil; nothing is gained from planting before late June in coastal areas and a little earlier inland. Plant when lilac flower buds are well developed. Seedlings can be thinned or transplanted later but it is better to sow thinly and save extra work. Some vegetables, like lettuce and beets, can be thinned and eaten. Large seeds, like peas, should be soaked overnight before planting to speed germination in late May and June, but it is usually not necessary if sown earlier. Parsnip takes a while to emerge and needs to be kept evenly moist; for this reason, some people place a board over the sown trench. Old parsnip seeds (one year or older) rarely germinate. Always check seed packages for special instructions about germination. Ignore dates and times. Start sowing seeds about two weeks after the snow has melted off the beds. You can always reseed in two to three weeks if something terrible happens to the first batch. Germination will be a little slow this early in the year, but you will get good plants; many vegetables do not do well unless planted early (e.g., onion sets and seedlings, broad beans, peas, and carrots).

Young plants can be planted when you want an early crop or when the vegetable requires a long growing season. The usual transplants are tomatoes, cabbage and relatives (cole crops), members of the melon family (cucumber, zucchini, squash, etc.), and onion seedlings. Start them according to the instructions given in Chapter 12 and harden them off before planting.

Special treatment can benefit your vegetables. I use fences on the windward side and grow peas on them. These fences (Figure 31) are made with two-by-twos for the frame (4 ft long by 3 ft high / 1.3 m by 1 m) with the side-pieces extended 1 foot (30 cm) to push down in the bed. A piece of 1-inch mesh (2.5 cm mesh) chicken wire is stapled to it. Such fences are effective. Cloches, small temporary shelters, are also useful. These can be small plastic-covered greenhouses that fit over about four tomato plants. Remove roof coverings after 1 July or the plants will get too hot; re-cover in September. You can also make tunnels; the frames are made of heavy wire or flexible 0.5-inch (1.2 cm) plastic water pipes bent in a U-shape (Figure 32). These can be pushed down in the soil or set in two boards. Old coat hangers can also be used. The covering can be a long strip of plastic (4 or 6 mil) or spun polyester. The sides can be buried in the soil and the ends gathered and held with a rock. On a bright day, open one or both ends. You need to keep the temperature from dropping too much at night and not have it get too much warmer than the outside temperature during the day. Gradually remove the tunnel in late June; however, some gardeners leave tunnels in place until harvest. This is useful for crops that like heat or at least warmer conditions (polyester fibre is porous, so overheating is not a danger) and/or when insect pests are a problem. Cole crops come through this treatment beautifully – my friend's broccoli was incredible.

Weeds should be kept under control; a few minutes work each day makes this easy. Make sure that roots and root shoulders are kept covered with soil. Mulch with grass clippings to maintain even moisture; moisture is essential for good growth and the prevention of cracked tomatoes. Watch for pests. Cans buried to their rims and loosely covered with small boards catch carpenters (sow bugs) and slugs, especially if you add beer or fruit juice. Empty regularly. I am not sure which does more damage, carpenters or slugs. Try to keep the spraying of chemicals to a minimum. I enjoy carrots above everything and am bothered by the carrot rust fly (its larvae tunnel all around the outside of the root and leave a network of black soil). A tunnel of spun polyester prevents this by keeping the adult flies out so that they cannot lay their eggs on the little carrots.

The following list of vegetables includes more comments than the lists in earlier chapters because it is important that your vegetables succeed. I will not give many recommendations because what vegetables grow well for me may not grow well for you. The best approach is to compare notes with other gardeners in your area, try a number of vegetables, and then try one or two different ones each year; keep notes. Soon you will have your own old reliables. The following types usually grow well for everyone without the gardener having to resort to heroic efforts.

Annual Crops

- Beans – a good productive crop. Do not plant seeds before the second (if you live in a warm location) or third week of June. Soil must be warm. Soak seeds overnight and use seed inoculant. Beans prefer a warm, sunny location. Harvest as they reach a mature size.

- Beets – seeds require a warm soil temperature to germinate; use a row cover after sowing. If your beets do not grow, add boron (1 oz borax in 4 gal water / 28 g borax in 16 l water) and wood ash (for potash) to the soil. Many varieties. Some gardeners like cylindra types for slicing; try Lutz Green Leaf (also called Winter Keeper) – huge, with good leaves and roots.

- Broad (or Fava) Beans – soak seeds overnight; plant about a week after the snow has gone. Tall plants with white and black flowers. Pods are the size of wieners; when opened, reveal lima-bean-like seeds embedded in plush. Boil and serve with melted butter and oregano. Snip off top after five trusses of flowers have formed.

- Brussels Sprouts and Broccoli – grow well but get cabbage butterfly caterpillars (use spun polyester fibre). Prefer rich organic soil (added compost gives best results) with a pH over 6. Start inside. Try Romanesco broccoli.

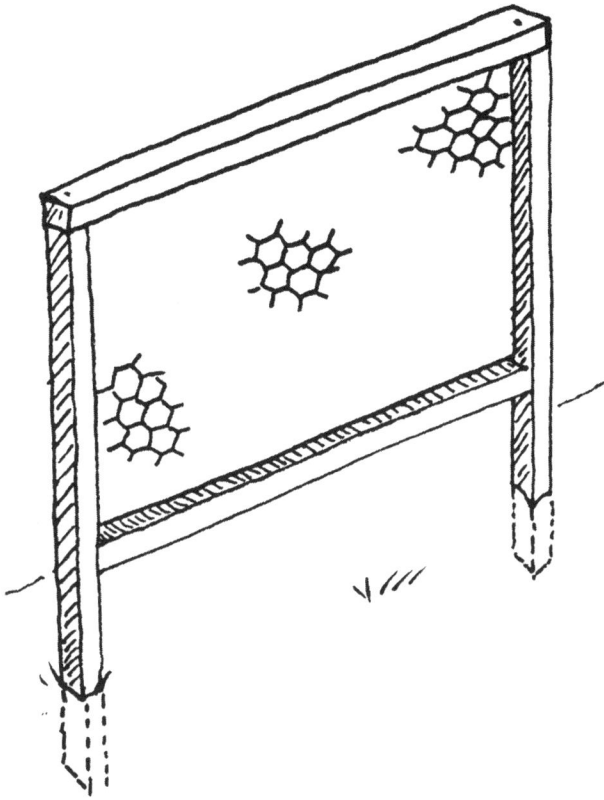

Figure 31. A sheltering fence.

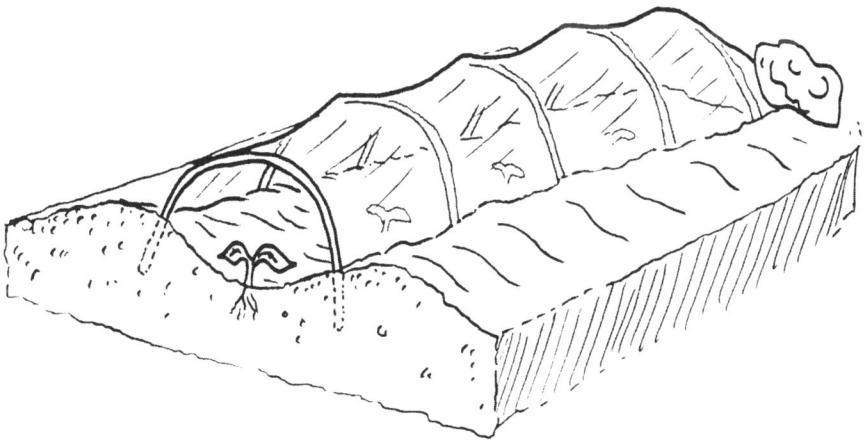

Figure 32. A framed protective tunnel made from spun polyester fibre.

- Cabbage – an old standby. Many types: early, winter keepers, savoy, purple. Start indoors. Protect from cabbage butterfly caterpillars.
- Carrots – plant seeds about a week or two after the snow has gone. Many types; try a variety. Soil should be kept evenly moist to avoid bitterness and splitting. Do not harvest too soon. After a hot, dry summer, carrots may be pencil-size in September but will become larger by late October.
- Cauliflower – tie leaves over developing curds to keep them white. Check catalogue descriptions. Start inside.
- Celery – start indoors (Chapter 12) and transplant to the garden. Needs adequate water supply for tasty stalks, or becomes bitter.
- Cucumbers – need a warm location. Lots of compost, start indoors, give them room to creep (it may be too cool for them on a trellis, except by a south-facing wall). Some varieties require male and female plants (check instructions on seed packages); use spun polyester fibre to cover.
- Endive – grow like lettuce.
- Green Bush Beans – many good varieties. I like Romano, a broad pod with a nice flavour.
- Leeks – start indoors and transplant outside about one to two weeks after the snow has disappeared. Plant in a trench so that you can cover the growing stem in order to get a long white eating portion.
- Lettuce – many varieties. Does better in moist locations away from the hot midday sun. Start some indoors for early salads; plant seeds in small beds every few weeks until early August for a succession of crops. Some varieties of lettuce seeds require light to germinate so just press them into loosened soil and keep moist.
- Onions – push sets (little bulbs grown from seed the previous year) into the ground about two weeks after the snow has gone. Seeds can be started indoors in February (traditionally, seeds were sown on Christmas or New Year's Day) and transplanted in mid-May. Generally, cooking onions are grown from sets, Spanish onions from seed. The size of an onion at harvest is determined by the number of days it has been growing before 21 June.

- Parsnips – sow in mid-April; harvesting after a few frosts improves the flavour. Loose soil allows large roots to form.
- Peas – snow peas and podded peas do well. Soak seeds overnight; plant in mid-April; use a seed inoculant to help them along.
- Potatoes – an East Coast staple. I have grown many varieties, all of which differ in taste, texture, shape, and skin and flesh colour. There is a potato for every purpose. After digging potatoes in the autumn I select egg-sized tubers from plants that have grown and produced well. Place them in labelled egg cartons; leave cartons open and store in a bright basement window for the winter. The tubers will turn green and send up short, stubby sprouts early in the new year. I dig deep trenches (9 in / 22.5 cm) with a vertical back to the north and bury the tubers just below the soil, spaced about 15 inches (36 cm). Fill in the trench as they grow. You can side-dress with compost or chemical fertilizer. Avoid lime, as it promotes scab, as does dry soil in the summer. Make sure that you get disease-free tubers and be prudent about using shared plants as you do not want to introduce canker or golden nematode to your garden. If your potatoes turn black when they are cooked (caused by excess iron in soil), add 1 teaspoon (5 ml) of vinegar to the cooking water.
- Radishes – sow seeds about a week after the snow melts and repeat seeding every two weeks. Do not grow well in hot weather, but you can plant again in late summer.
- Scarlet Runner Beans – seeds should be soaked and sown in late April or early May. Climb to about 6 feet (2 m). Succession of beans through the summer. Pick pods while young, as they tend to get stringy.
- Spinach – sow seeds every 10 to 14 days after the snow melts until early June, then from mid-August onwards. Mulch helps keep the wrinkled leaves free of grit. Cut outer leaves with a sharp knife; the harvest continues until the plants bolt (start flowering).
- Squash – some squash get carried away and cover huge expanses of garden. Sweet Mama Winter Squash and Spirit Pumpkin are favourites. Plant seeds indoors in mid-May. Give them lots of compost and stand back.

- Summer Turnip – rarely grown by gardeners on the East Coast. Delicious.
- Swiss Chard – a delicious green. If you are experiencing problems in growing swiss chard you may need to add lime, as chard does not do well in acidic soil. Harvest outer leaves with a knife and let the plant continue to grow.
- Tomatoes – with extra care tomatoes can be grown outside. Try a number of varieties in your garden; Toy Boy, Scotia, and Sub-arctic Maxi varieties do well. Start indoors (Chapter 12). Put 1 teaspoon (5 ml) of Epsom salts in each planting hole to increase yields. Rich soil and lots of heat are the secret to success. Mulch. Even moisture is essential or the fruit will crack.
- Turnip/Rutabaga – East Coast turnips are superlative. The traditional variety is Laurentian. Sow in late April or early May and thin seedlings; these are edible. Turnip tops are the young plants of rape and are planted in April.
- Yellow Wax Beans – delicious.
- Zucchini – and other summer squashes grow well. I plant seeds outside in mid-June in a warm location and have had better success than with transplants. Harvest fruit before they get too big, which happens quickly.

Perennial Crop

Asparagus – prepare a separate bed in a sheltered location and dig deeply. They are heavy feeders, so use lots of compost or manure initially and top dress annually. Buy roots in the spring or plant seeds. It takes several years before the spears become thick, but it is worth the effort as the taste of home-grown asparagus is wonderful.

Greenhouse Crops

Many crops benefit from the extra shelter of a greenhouse. The important points of greenhouse culture are ventilation (Figure 33), heat control, and water. As small greenhouses are difficult to control, try to have one at least 10 feet by 15 feet (3 m by 5 m). Both ends should be capable of being opened so that air can circulate; otherwise your

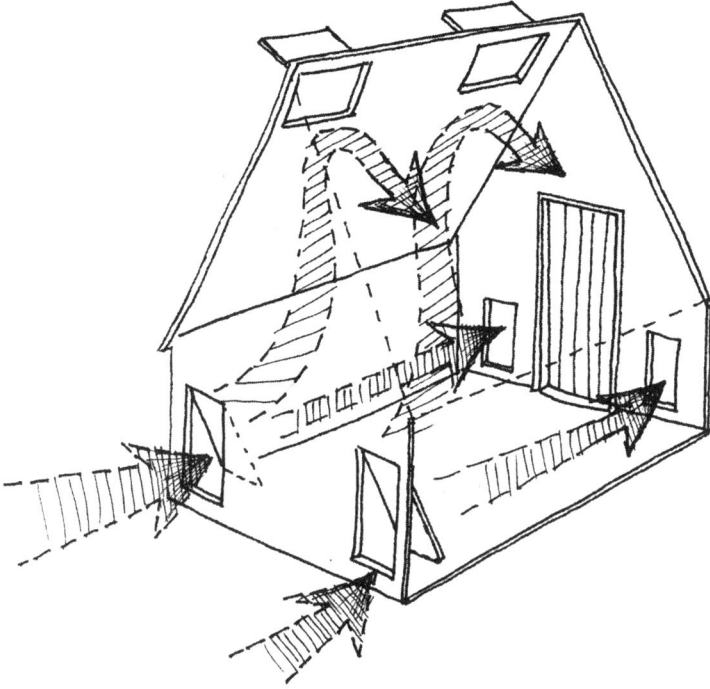

Figure 33. Ensure greenhouses have ample ventilation.

plants will develop fungal diseases. A greenhouse also needs vents in the roof; these vents should remain open throughout the summer and closed at night during the early and late parts of the growing season. Greenhouses should feel comfortable, not hot and steamy. Try to keep the temperature between 60° and 85°F (15°-25°C). A large box fan may need to be installed during the summer. Heating cables (the type sold for running along eaves to prevent ice build-up can be used) can be buried in the soil to help growth both early and late in the season. Warm roots are essential for good growth. Water with tepid water early in the morning and again after lunch, if required. Plant leaves should never be wet, especially in the evening.

Cucumbers – as the shoots climb, install chicken wire on the north wall of the greenhouse so they do not shade other plants.

Tomatoes – many gardeners build greenhouses solely to grow tomatoes. Try several varieties, not necessarily greenhouse varieties, and see what you like. The flavour of fresh, home-grown tomatoes is wonderful.

Herbs

Many groups of herbs are grown for different purposes and sometimes the same plant fits several categories, including food additives, teas, potpourris, and dyes.

The flavours we desire in cooking are due to essential oils in the herbaceous parts of plants and seeds. These oils are volatile and so are easily lost. They are produced in high concentrations under slight stress conditions. To obtain the best flavours, grow herbs in sunny locations. Some herbs can be grown among vegetables, others with flowers, in tubs on patios, and in special herb gardens.

Herbs do not require unusual growing conditions – a good garden soil with adequate moisture, regular fertilizer application, and weeding is sufficient. As with any gardening, add compost, humus, and leaves. Space the plants. Use a mulch of grass clippings to conserve moisture and reduce weeds. Start small. Build gradually.

Spend the winter with catalogue descriptions and design a garden; as leaf textures and colours vary in herbs, this can be included in the design. Make sure that the plants can be reached easily for harvesting, even on wet days.

If you plant a basic set of herbs with your vegetables, select only annuals. Plant perennials like rhubarb and strawberries in a separate bed.

Annual culinary herbs – parsley, basil, nasturtium, anise, dill, borage, chervil, coriander, and summer savory.

Perennial culinary herbs – sage, thyme, chives, and mint (control, or it spreads over the garden).

Special Herb Gardens

The most famous of special herb gardens, the Elizabethan knot garden, used hedges of shrubby plants like lavender and *Santolina* to make designs based on knots. Colour, texture, ground cover (plants or crushed stone) to make the patterns stand out, and careful pruning are essential concerns. A knot garden needs to be located so that it can be seen from above.

Dye gardens are often used by craftspeople, and, since large

Figure 34. Place special herb gardens in an easily accessible location.

quantities of herbs are needed, this type of garden may be laid out in clumps and rows.

Fragrance gardens are a delight. Plant fragrant plants near a patio, garden bench, or by the front door (Figure 34).

Kitchen gardens not only should be pleasing to the eye, but also functional. Plant your herb garden so that it is easily accessible from the kitchen. Easy access to all plants should be considered in the design so that acrobatics with knives and scissors are minimized. Mulches are also important to keep the leaves clean.

A basic herb garden could include parsley, chives, a few onions for their leaves, Egyptian onions, sage, basil, thyme, dill, borage, mints, nasturtium, and, over the summer, pots of rosemary and bay.

Containers are often used for growing herbs as they can be conveniently positioned; they are particularly appropriate for apartment dwellers. The containers should be sufficiently large so that they do not dry out in a short time. Half-barrels, or something constructed of wood, work well. A layer of peat mixed with lime placed in the bottom to soak up excess water so that it does not flow everywhere acts as a reservoir. Fill containers with potting soil. Fertilize regularly. In the winter, store the containers in a shed or garage or at least cover them with plastic so that they do not fill with water and freeze. In the spring scrape out the top 6 inches of soil and re-fill with a mixture of potting mix and manure.

Collecting and Preserving Herbs

Ideally, fresh herbs should be used in the summer, but they can also be preserved for use in the winter. The essential oils must be remembered. Dry in a shaded, cool place with adequate air circulation. Do not use any moldy plants. When the plants are thoroughly dry, crumble the leaves and store in an airtight jar in a cool, dry, dark place.

That is the traditional method; however, freezers have changed all that as dried herbs can be stored airtight in the freezer. Fresh herbs can be frozen and stored in plastic bags or serving-size amounts frozen in ice cubes and stored in labelled bags.

Store herbs in oil for up to nine months. Alternate layers of leaves and olive oil in a jar. Drain off the oil as you use the herbs and use it for barbecuing, sautéing, marinating, and in salad dressings.

Herbal Teas

Boil water. Use dried herbs. Experiment. Try 2 teaspoons dried herbs per cup. Steep for 5-10 minutes. If desired, add honey and/or lemon; milk clouds flavour. Use balm, basil, catnip, elderberry flowers, fennel, fenugreek, hibiscus, mint, oswego tea, chamomile, rose hip, or yarrow. Try fresh clover flowers.

Culinary Use of Herbs

Herbs and spices should complement the ingredients in a preparation: they enhance, not dominate, taste. When you try a new recipe, follow it carefully. Do not modify it out-of-hand or all your food will taste the same. To become familiar with the use of herbs in cooking, use standard recipes and get a taste for which herbs go with which foods. Before long, inspiration will guide your hand in seasoning.

Herb-Flavoured Condiments

Fresh herbs can be used in vinegar, jelly, butter, or sugar. These preparations make good gifts.

Herb Vinegar – use tarragon, sage, thyme, marjoram, basil, savory, and dill alone or in combination. Use rosemary and mint in a vinegar for fruit salads. Put several shoots in a bottle with a non-metal cap. Fill with vinegar (1 pint / 0.5 l). Keep in a warm place to steep for three weeks or to taste. Strain. Add a fresh sprig for decoration.

Herb Jelly – make apple jelly. For 2 cups of liquid: add 1/4 cup chopped fresh rosemary, sage, or thyme leaves, or add 1/2 cup chopped spearmint, basil, or lemon verbena leaves just before final boil. Strain and bottle. Quick method: warm store-bought jelly in a pan of warm water, stir in herbs. Store in refrigerator. For a more subtle flavour, put a leaf or two of rose geranium, scarlet bergamot, or lemon balm in the jar before pouring in apple jelly. Use mint jelly for young meats. Baste pork, chicken, or veal with thyme, sage, or rosemary jelly during the last 20 minutes of roasting.

Herb Butter – bring 1/4 pound butter to room temperature, cream, blend in about 1/4 cup of freshly chopped herbs (less of sage and rosemary); add 1 tablespoon lemon juice. For garlic butter, use 1 tablespoon chopped garlic and 3 tablespoons chopped fresh parsley. Wrap butter in plastic wrap, chill, form into a roll, freeze or refrigerate.

Herb Sugar – add 2 tablespoons chopped scented rose petals or balm, rose geranium, or mint leaves to 1 cup of sugar. Store in airtight container for six weeks. Use with tea, on plain cookies, or in simple desserts.

Basic Herb Cooking

Fresh and dried herbs differ slightly in flavour. Substitute 1 tablespoon of crumbled or 1/4 teaspoon powdered dried herbs for 1 tablespoon of fresh. Use frozen or oil-prepared herbs in the same quantities as fresh.

Heat releases the oils that provide flavour. Bring cold dishes to room temperature before serving. Bruise herbs before adding to cold drinks to release their flavours. When cooking, add herbs near the end, as prolonged cooking destroys flavours. Add sprigs of mint as an attractive garnish and a subtle flavouring.

Traditional Herb Preparations

- Bouquet garni – tie together four sprigs of parsley, two sprigs of thyme, and one bay leaf. Remove before serving.
- Fines herbes – equal parts of minced parsley, chervil, tarragon, and chives.
- Garam masala – cinnamon, cardamom, cloves, cumin seeds, coriander seeds, and black peppercorns.

Caution: mixing too many herbs can result in a bitter or nondescript flavour.

"Plants never read gardening manuals, so they rarely behave as you expect."

Notes

Chapter 11
Fruits and Berries

Fruit was grown much more widely in the past before quick trans-world shipment of produce. Some gardeners struggle to grow apples and pears, but I would recommend that you start out with small fruits such as currants and strawberries. There are areas of the East Coast where apples grow well but there are several problems associated with apples on a small lot: they are magnets for children at harvest time; and small to medium apple trees take a beating in the winter and lose many limbs to sinking snow.

Small fruit plants require good soil preparation. Beds for them should be situated so that they receive lots of sun. These beds should be devoted to this purpose for ease of management and picking. A generous portion of well-rotted manure or compost should be applied to the beds each spring.

Pruning can make all the difference to crop production and will be discussed for each type of fruit.

Harvesting should not be done until the fruit is ripe. I usually wait until fruit starts to drop from the plant or, in the case of strawberries, when it parts easily from the plant. Gooseberries, especially, are usually picked too soon, before they have developed their wonderful flavour. Most small fruit grow close to the ground and I pick them while sitting on my empty 1-gallon paint tin.

Small Fruit

- Blackberries – great thorny masses of stems, but what a fruit! Given a warm, sheltered location and a large amount of compost or manure, these produce their succulent fruit on two-year-old canes. There is a thornless variety, but it is not hardy.

- Currants, Black – old standbys. Most varieties do well. The secret with black currants is compost in the spring, and pruning. Each stem grows up from the ground one year, produces for three or four years, and then should be cut to the ground as soon as the snow has gone in the spring. I once overheard two older ladies talking about making black currant jam and one proclaimed that, to prevent the skins from going tough, sugar must be added at the end of cooking – and she is right. This advice applies to all varieties of currants and gooseberries.

- Currants, Red and White – grown like black currants; pruning is different because the stems will produce fruit for more years. Cut stems to the ground after five years or when fruit production on a stem decreases. Some varieties of red currants produce abundantly. Pick white currants before they turn reddish (which they do when overripe) for best colour in jellies or drinks.

- Gooseberries – red, white, and yellow; large and small (Figure 35). Fruit have a thick "skin," so larger fruit have more soft flesh. Rich soil, sun, and moisture are needed. Prune as for red currants.

- Raspberries – grow abundantly in the wild but it is nice to have some fruit handy in the garden (Figure 36). Usually planted in rows so that you can run wires along each side to keep the canes upright (Figure 37). Raspberries send up shoots one year, and these bear fruit the next year. In the spring, don gloves and cut those stems that bore fruit the previous summer to the ground. Make sure that stems do not become crowded. Top dress with compost or manure. Pick and enjoy. There are several single harvest varieties of red raspberry that ripen at different times in the growing season; these are good for preserves. There are also ever-bearing varieties which yield fruit over a longer period and are nice for an occasional meal. In addition to red, there are yellow and black raspberries.

Figure 35. Gooseberries.

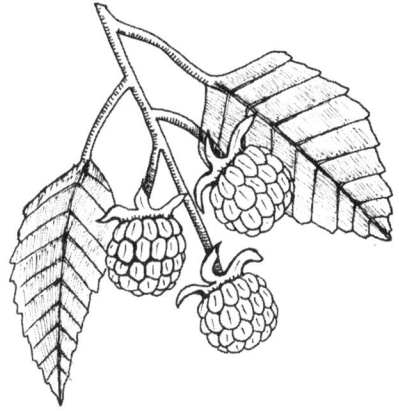

Figure 36. Raspberries.

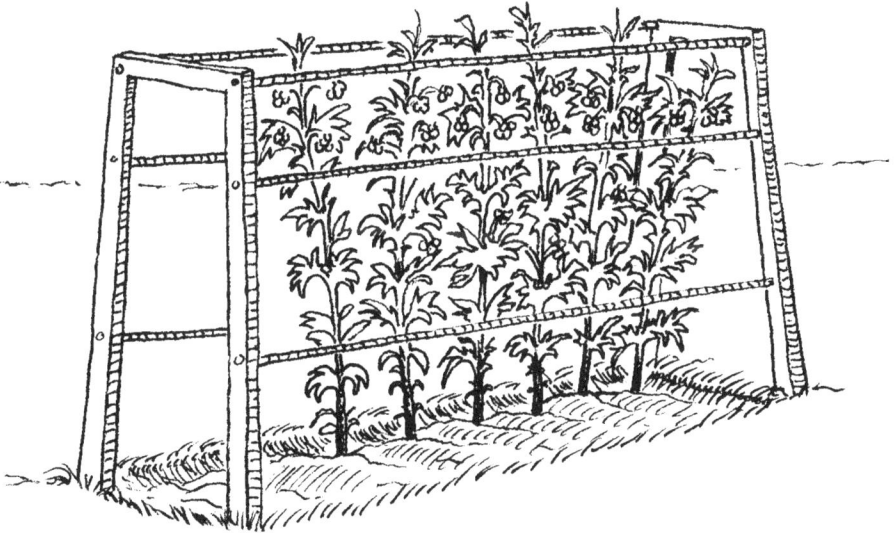

Figure 37. Raspberry canes require support.

- Strawberries – I feel that strawberries should never be eaten if more than a second off the plant (Figure 38), so dessert involves sitting on the grass and eating, with the sun shining, fluffy clouds overhead, and birds singing! Strawberries also go well with cream and bubbly. Plant them in rows. Do not bury the crown (where the new leaves arise). Start with certified plants from nurseries, as viruses pose

Figure 38. Strawberries.

a problem. In much of North America, with the exception of northerly areas such as Newfoundland, people have to replant strawberries every few years because of the build-up of viruses in the plants. If you buy strawberries from a nursery, they usually come in a bundle with bare roots; soak the roots in tepid water for several hours before planting. I do not bother picking off the flowers the first year. If the plant is strong, it will produce fruit; otherwise, it will not. Traditionally, straw was placed between the rows, but in parts of the East Coast, any moisture-retaining material also retains slugs and carpenters, which devour the berries.

The best plan is to have three sections in your strawberry patch: producing rows, growing rows, and new rows. The new rows are planted with small plants produced by the runners; they grow during the second year, and then produce for a few years. Start a new row about every two years. Fence them in, as runners head out in all directions. Rich soil, a sunny location, and evenly retained moisture give good crops. Try an ever-bearing variety with single crop varieties, as they bear fruit from early in the season until late autumn.

Tree Fruit

Fruit trees are often damaged in winter and fruit do not always ripen. Apples and pears seem to be particularly subject to winter damage.

Several types of fruit trees are recommended:

- Apples – growing them espaliered (on a trellis against a wall) avoids some winter damage. Cortland is a good variety.

- Cherries – sour red cherries do well, but sweet cherries do not unless grown in a warm location. If you decide to grow sweet cherries, plant two different varieties for pollination or you will not get any, or much, fruit. Black Knot, which often originates on wild trees, is a fungal disease that produces black lumpy knobs on the branches of cherry trees. The affected branches should be cut off several inches to the trunk-side of the lump and burned. Prevention can be effected by spraying with powdered sulphur, just as the leaf buds start to open. Fire blight, another fungal disease, has been killing cherries in recent years.

- Pears – grow them as you would apples.

- Plums – they grow well on the East Coast and there are many new varieties, in addition to the reliable Damson. Two different varieties, at least, need to be planted for pollination and fruit-set. Catalogues usually provide directions. Black Knot is also a problem (see Cherries).

"Experiment with new varieties and types of plants.
This is the real joy of gardening."

Notes

Chapter 12
Seeds and Cuttings

One of the fascinations of gardening is seeing life start. This can be achieved from seeds or cuttings, and these techniques are used for adding plants to your collection or propagating your present plants.

Seeds

Seeds are produced by plants to enable the species to over-winter, in the case of annuals, or to survive unfavourable conditions, which might result from a trip to a new locale or a period of bad weather. I mention this because special conditions must sometimes be provided for seeds to germinate after their dormancy. Although most seeds can be planted at our convenience, some need to feel that they have been through winter – so a few nights (and days) in a freezer will do the trick: pansies, violas, and primroses need this treatment. Others, like rose seeds, need an actual winter, so they must be planted in damp sand and frozen for a minimum of three months. Others, like holly, need two winters, so must be planted in the garden and carefully marked. After a cold treatment, these seeds can be planted in the normal fashion. Some seeds, like poppies and several varieties of lettuce, need light to germinate. These seeds should be pressed into the soil and kept evenly moist. Always check seed packages for special instructions. Use a stick or strips cut from a plastic bottle (like a bleach bottle) to label the container with the variety and sowing date.

Seeds Indoors

Plant in trays, pots, empty food containers, or whatever is available. Just be sure there are holes in the bottom for drainage. These containers should be deep enough not to dry out because, if seedlings dry, they die. Three inches (7.5 cm) of soil is the minimum. It should be screened to eliminate lumps, as seedling roots are delicate. The soil into which the seeds are sown should be fine to ensure good contact and even moisture to the seeds. Germination involves the seed absorbing water, sending out a root, and then a shoot. Large seeds can be given a boost by soaking overnight before planting. Heat is required for germination, and, even though a plant may come from the arctic, its seeds germinate best at 20-25°C, which is the temperature on top of a refrigerator.

Once the seeds are up, they should be placed in cooler conditions. If the plants are to be put outside later, the best temperature for seedlings is around 15°C. The danger at this temperature is losing the seedlings to damping off, a fungal disease that rots the seedling at the soil level. This can be avoided by spacing the seedlings well, keeping the soil just moist (not wet), and providing good ventilation (a small fan operating continuously nearby). If you still have problems, use a weak solution of chlorine bleach (1-2 tbsp / gal [15-30 ml / 4 l water]) to water the seedling flats once or twice.

Seedlings grow quickly and, if they do not have sufficient light, they shoot up tall and stringy. They must be grown in a south-facing basement window or in a cool room under fluorescent lights. Although fluorescent lights appear to be very bright, they have almost no effect on seedling growth when placed more than 8 inches (20 cm) above the plant leaves.

To start seeds use a fluorescent light fixture with a canopy to focus all the light onto the plants and timer on a stand (Figure 39). Most growers use a combination of fluorescent tubes – one cool white and one daylight, or one cool white and one wide-spectrum Grolux©. After planting the seeds, hang the fluorescent fixtures so that the tubes are 4 to 6 inches (10-15 cm) above the soil. Raise the lights as the seedlings grow so that the lights are about 6 inches (15 cm) above the leaves and the seedlings remain sturdy. Keep the lights on for 14 to 16 hours a day. It is also a good idea to operate a small fan continuously while you are growing the seedlings.

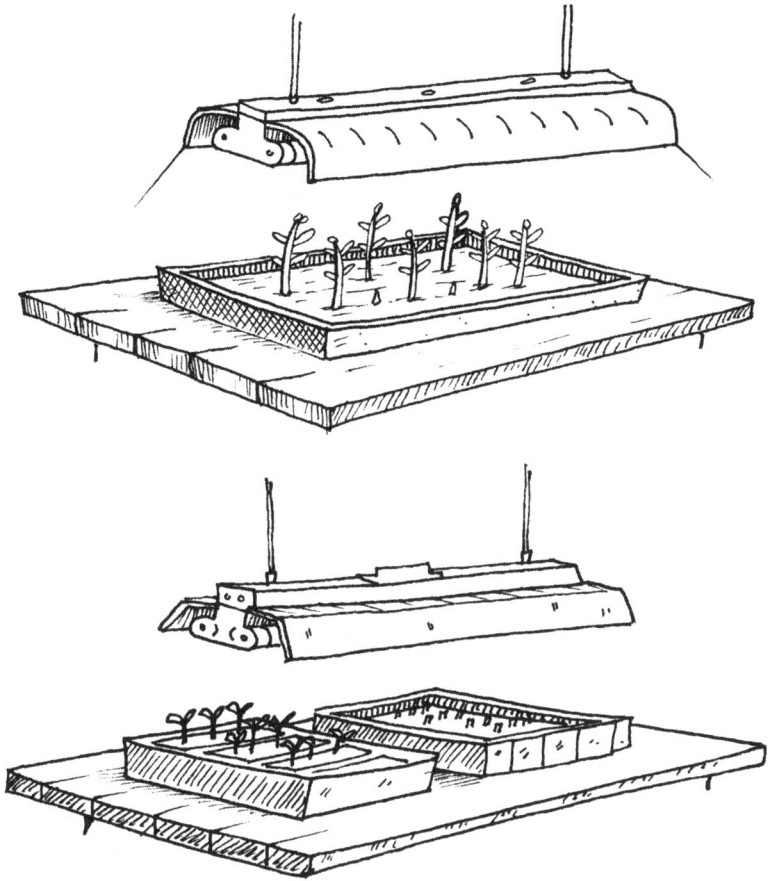

Figure 39. Starting seedlings under fluorescent lights.

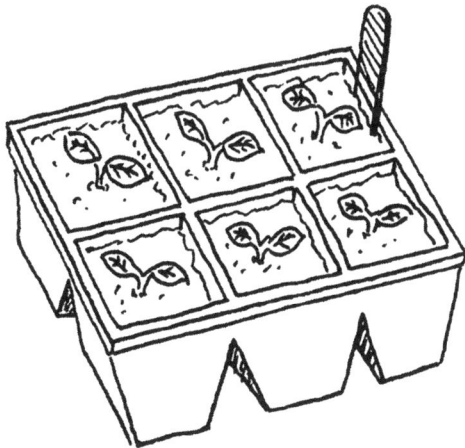

Figure 40. A seedling flat.

It is best to sow the seeds thinly so that they do not need transplanting. I use trays with flats that fit in them, with individual compartments for the plants (Figure 40). It is better to sow two seeds and pull out the extra seedling, carefully, or snip it off with small, pointed sewing scissors. If you want seedlings to grow on because they are special in some way, plant them in pots and then "prick" them out into the trays just mentioned. A toothpick, penknife, or some pointed object will help. The seedling should have its two seed leaves and the first true leaf just coming when you transplant them. Do not over- or under-pot or let the seedlings dry out. Do not panic! When the seedlings get larger, they can be put in 3-inch and then 4-inch pots and so on. The tendency is to keep the largest and sturdiest seedlings and this is fine for a single variety, but, from a mixed package, the smaller seedlings and late germinators are often the choicest colours.

Fertilizing should be kept to a minimum, as lush growth is difficult to harden off. Use a fertilizer with higher second and third numbers (e.g., 4-8-8). Use one-quarter the recommended strength every week.

Timing is everything. Do not start your plants too soon or you will end up with tangles of snakes. Six weeks before you expect to transplant them to the garden is plenty of time. Certain plants like snapdragons and petunias, shrubs and some perennials, and other slower-growing plants may need to be started earlier. Onions and leeks are traditionally sown on Christmas (or New Year's) Day. Harden off your seedlings about one to two weeks before transplanting.

Hardening Off

This involves sending the little seedlings off into the cruel world of cold wind and bright light. There are elaborate structures (cold frames) for sheltering seedlings, but a cardboard box, well-battened down, will do. For a week or so keep the box in a cool garage or shed at night, then put it out by the house each morning, and open. Gradually expose seedlings to outdoor conditions and protect from extremes. Watch for scorching (the leaves turn reddish – too much sun, too soon), wind burn (dry, beige patches on the leaves – protect from the wind), or drying out (shrivelled and limp – keep watered). In this manner, seedlings are gradually weaned to the real world.

Transplanting is described in Chapter 7. Water the seedlings well as soon as they are stuck in the soil, and shelter for a few days. Be prepared to protect them during late frosts.

Cuttings

Some plants are easily propagated by cuttings. The resulting plants are clones, thus identical to the original plant.

Rooting a cutting requires a branch of a plant, or a leaf in some cases, and a moist place for roots to develop. Young branches are usually used with commonly rooted types. There is a proper method to root almost any type of plant, but most gardeners do not have the necessary special equipment. Trees and shrubs require more equipment (such as mist frames) and skill than most gardeners have. Most perennials are increased by dividing the roots and crown; however, pinks can be rooted from stem cuttings. Houseplants are the main object of our cutting efforts. If you particularly want to propagate a woody plant, try layering it. Refer to more detailed gardening books or the Internet for methods.

Cuttings are taken from the tips of branches so that the tissue is young and soft. Use a sharp razor blade to avoid crushing the stem or leaving jagged bits. Make a clean cut, on a slight angle, halfway between the third and fourth leaves from the tip (Figure 41). Rooting can be done in water: use a dark jar (dark-coloured or covered with foil), although the plants rarely fuss, filled with lukewarm water. Keep the bottom portion of the stem covered with water and, when there are a dozen or so roots 1 inch (2.5 cm) long, pot them. Research has shown that placing willow twigs in with cuttings accelerates rooting.

Cuttings can also be rooted in your favourite potting mixture. Make a hole in the soil with a pencil and gently put the cut end of a stem into the hole (Figure 42). Firm the soil around it to ensure good contact between cutting and soil. Since the cutting has no roots, it must be covered with a plastic bag to prevent it from drying out. It is best to prepare the pot of soil ahead of time so that the soil is moist, not too wet or too dry. Do not close the bag tightly. Place this little rooting greenhouse in a warm place (74°F / 22°C) and watch that it does not dry out. It should be rooted in three or four weeks (test by very gently

Figure 41. Taking a cutting.

Figure 42. A fresh cutting in a pot of soil.

Figure 43. Use a sharp razor to cut and trim an African Violet cutting.

Figure 44. A planted African Violet cutting.

pulling on the stem – if it comes easily, wait; if it resists, it has rooted). After the cutting has rooted, over the next week gradually roll down the plastic bag to acclimatize the plant to room conditions. Succulents and other fleshy plants do not usually need a plastic covering. Because geraniums are susceptible to blackleg, a fungal disease which turns the stem black as it rots, cuttings should be placed on the counter for four to five hours so that the cut end heals (indicated by a beige or whitish film over the cut end). Proceed as above but do not cover with plastic.

Leaves of some plants, especially African Violets, can be used to start new ones. Cut the leaf stalk at an angle (Figure 43) and put it in the soil (Figure 44). Small plantlets emerge in about six to eight weeks. Leaves of Rex Begonias (planted with the leaf stalk down in the soil so that the point where it joins the leaf is touching the soil) will produce new plants, and leaves of several succulent houseplants, like the Jade Plant (*Crassula*), grow new plantlets if the stem end of the leaf is simply nestled into the soil surface.

*"If a plant is sick or growing poorly, do it and yourself
a favour – discard it."*

Notes

Chapter 13
Houseplants

Some people feel that autumn is the time to sit back and relax from gardening, but many of us, myself included, then start our indoor gardens. Many lovely foliage plants bloom all winter. Geraniums which have been summered outdoors are full of buds (not bugs! – although there can be, so check) that bloom in profusion through winter. Holiday cacti, including the Christmas cactus, bloom from Thanksgiving to Easter. There are bulbs like hyacinths and tulips to be forced and other bulbs like amaryllis to be bloomed. Of course, African Violets never quit, or should not.

I have heard a number of people say that they want a plant to brighten a dark corner. A few plants struggle under these conditions. The famous cast-iron plant (*Aspidistra*) and snake plant (*Sansevieria*) linger on for years, but, given a chance, they are wonderful. I had a large pot of snake plants in my south-facing picture window and every February they bloomed – pale greenish-yellow flowers with a wonderful hyacinth-like fragrance which wafted about the room at suppertime. Lamps and aquariums are what you should use to brighten a dark corner.

Growing conditions inside a house cannot usually be changed, but if you understand which conditions make a difference to plants then you can select types that do well under your particular conditions.

It is important to consider the conditions in your house: light, temperature, and humidity. You may not be able or want to change them, but you can work with them. They will affect your choice of soil, pot, and watering regime.

Temperature

The temperature of most homes is usually 15-25°C (50-83°F). Many people turn the heat down at night or put their plants in windows where it is a little cooler; this benefits the plants, as long as it does not get too cold. On cold nights years ago, plants were placed on a table in the centre of a room and covered with newspaper, or newspaper was placed between the plant and the windowpane.

Light

Light varies with the exposure and type of window. Each pane of glass reduces the amount of light passing through it; sheer curtains do the same. As morning sun is the best light, an east- or southeast-facing window is excellent (Figure 45). A south-facing window is good in the winter but may be too hot and bright in the summer; however, a sheer curtain drawn at midday helps. A south-facing window is good for geraniums, cacti, and succulents (cacti and succulents need regular watering while they are growing – see later in chapter).

North-facing windows are good locations for many plants, including ferns, begonias, Impatiens, and a broad range of foliage plants. Let the plants tell you their light requirements. If they turn pale, they are getting too much light (or not enough fertilizer). If they are spindly, they need more light.

Humidity

Humidity depends upon the type of heating system and the presence or absence of an air exchanger. Electric heat is the most difficult to manage. Plants need about 65 percent humidity; this can be achieved with containers of water placed around the plants. A misting with water early in the morning helps. You get to check over the plants and perk them up at the same time. Air circulation stimulates growth and prevents some common diseases encountered in houseplants. Forced air furnaces and air exchangers keep air moving, but for other systems your plants may need some assistance. Bay windows or large hot windows may benefit from a small fan, if many plants are grown there.

Now, a general word about living plants – the basics of growing houseplants. Roots grow through the potting mixture, where they absorb water and nutrients. They need oxygen to do this, so the soil mixture must not be dense or waterlogged. The stem takes water and nutrients up to the leaves and flowers, and food down to the roots. It holds the leaves up to the light, which is essential for photosynthesis (the manufacture of food). Because stems grow to the light, a plant must be turned regularly, in the house, to achieve symmetrical growth. The tip of the stem grows in preference to any of the side branches; to get branching and, thus, a bushy plant, pinch out the tip when the plant is short. Do not wait until the spindly cane of your rubber tree reaches the ceiling; cut off the tip when the plant is 12 to 18 inches (30-45 cm) tall.

Potting

Potting is the make-or-break point of growing houseplants. Happy roots make a happy plant. If the roots dry, the plants die.

Pots are usually plastic; they should have holes in the bottom and saucers to catch excess water. Large pots without holes can be managed but they are a constant worry. Pot size is determined by plant size. If you can imagine the volume of the plant that you want to re-pot (excluding roots), the pot should be one-third that size. Another way to consider this: the diameter of the top of the pot (imprinted on the bottoms of most plastic pots) should be one-third the height of the plant above the soil. Do not over-pot (put it in too large a pot). Problems arise with the soil getting too wet, the roots not getting enough air, and the roots then rotting – causing the plant to wilt – which makes the owner pour on more water until the plant is dead.

Make certain that the pot is clean. Wash in a solution of one part chlorine bleach to nine parts water.

Rough rocks can be placed over the holes in the bottom of a pot to prevent soil from washing out, but I simply push the soil in and proceed from there. Some people put a disc of paper towel in the bottom of the pot.

Figure 45. Ideally, houseplants should be placed in east- or southeast-facing windows.

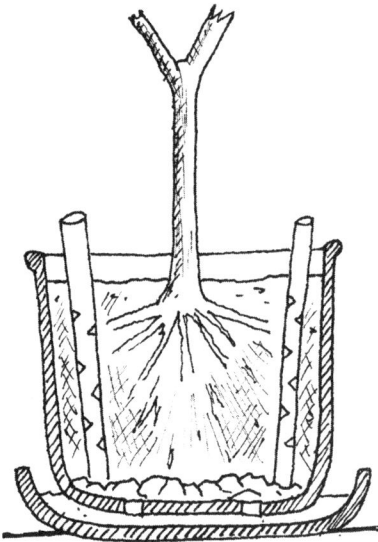

Figure 46. Large pots require notched pipes or straws for ventilation.

Figure 47. A newly re-potted houseplant.

Pots that are 12 or more inches (30 cm) in diameter need some extra care to prevent waterlogging and sour soil (Figure 46). I put several cups of activated charcoal (sold for aquarium filters) in the bottom. I take some 0.5-inch (1.2 cm) PVC (polyvinyl chloride) water pipe (not copper, as it can be toxic) and cut notches along its length. Put two or more of these notched pipe lengths in each pot so they extend from just above the soil level to the bottom. This keeps the soil aerated.

Opinions about potting soil can vary. Try a readily available mixture of soil. If plants do not grow well, try another, but give them at least six months to respond. Make no decisions after a week! Potting mixtures rarely contain soil any more. Heavy bags often contain sand and lighter bags contain mostly peat. Peat has disadvantages for home use. Nurseries use peat because it is light and inexpensive and, because of its porous nature, can be watered fairly often. In the home, however, peat dries surprisingly quickly and the plants die. Potted azaleas are particularly susceptible. A little liquid detergent (not dishwasher detergent) wets the peat, but I prefer to re-pot nursery plants using my own soil mixture.

The potting mixture I use consists of three parts commercial potting soil to one part horticultural grade vermiculite and one part perlite. I also add 1 tablespoon of agricultural lime. I use a 4-inch pot (but any container will do) to measure these ingredients into a large plastic bag: grip both ends firmly, shake well to mix thoroughly without creating dust.

Make certain the soil has been pasteurized; you do not want bugs or pests. If you are not confident that the soil has been sterilized, steam it in a container such as an old roaster or a roasting bag. Make sure that the soil is moist, and place the container in a 200°F (93°C) oven for four hours.

To re-pot, take a clean pot, one size larger (usually 1 in / 2.5 cm) than the present pot, and put some potting mixture in the bottom (Figure 47). Remove the plant from its old pot, disturbing the roots as little as possible. If it does not slip out, slip the stem between your first and second fingers to secure it, and, to keep the soil from spilling everywhere, turn the plant bottom up and tap the pot against the edge of table to free the plant. Use a small pot or scoop to add more potting mix to the bottom of the new pot until the root-ball is at the same level in the new pot as it was in the old pot. Fill in around the root-ball and firm the soil. Water well.

Watering

People always ask how often they should water their plants. Wrong question. You should ask: how do I know when my plant needs watering? Moist soil feels cool to the fingertip, while dry soil feels warm. Weather is one factor that affects how quickly the soil dries out. Another point to consider is the state of the plant: it needs more water when it is actively growing, and less when it is not. Many plants do not grow much in winter and, with dull cool days, water should be reduced. As the days lengthen, look for new leaves, and, when they start, gradually increase the water. I like to leave the water in the watering can for a day or so; it is important that the water be lukewarm. It is best to water in the morning on a sunny day, but do not wait for that if the plant needs water. Some plant leaves, like those of African Violets, develop brown spots if cold water is allowed to stand on them; so keep the leaves dry. Blot any drops of water with a paper towel.

Fertilizing

Houseplants do not need much fertilizer but, since peat-based potting mixtures contain few nutrients, a regular fertilizing program will help. Ideally, I try to use a fertilizer at one-quarter the recommended dose every week or two. Most commercial houseplant fertilizers are good, but, because they each contain different micronutrients, I buy several and alternate them. The trio of numbers on fertilizers (e.g., 20-20-20) indicates the proportions of nitrogen-phosphorus-potassium, the major nutrients required for plant growth. Nitrogen promotes leaf growth, phosphorus flowering, and potassium general growth. Other macronutrients and micronutrients are included in the fertilizer. Agricultural lime adds minerals as well as adjusts the pH, which is important as it helps the plants take up nutrients.

Special Indoor Gardening Techniques

Window sills are suitable, at least after they are widened in newer homes, but sometimes you want to grow many more than will fit by your windows.

For fluorescent-light gardens, use commercially available fluorescent light stands, or make your own (see Chapter 12 for information on growing under lights). The type of tubes used, the distance of the fluorescent tubes from the leaves, the temperature, and air circulation are important factors in growing with fluorescent light. Some low-growing begonias (e.g., Rex Begonias), African Violets, and gloxinias and their relatives are well suited to this type of growing.

Hydroponics involves a container filled with a nutrient solution that is recirculated or aerated with an aquarium air pump. This system is used for growing herbs, lettuce, and other food crops in windows or under lights. It is fairly straightforward, but read up on the topic to decide if you want to invest in the equipment and time for this type of gardening.

Common Houseplant Problems

The best method to prevent problems is to quarantine all plant material that you bring into your house, including garden plants, potted plants, gift plants, cut flowers, and flower arrangements. It can take as much as two months for some pests to show up. Nursery-grown plants are regularly sprayed with pesticides, but insect eggs often remain on the plants.

Wilting – wilting often occurs even though a plant has been given plenty of water, particularly in winter and spring when the plants are not actively growing and the days are grey and cool. Too much water rots the roots; the plant cannot draw up water, and it wilts. More water worsens the situation. The solution: keep the soil just moist, move the plant back from the window, and spray with water every morning and noon. It should recover and start growing again in a few weeks.

Spots on Leaves – wet, brown spots on plant leaves are usually caused by fungi and bacteria. The plant is probably weakened by improper conditions, too moist or too cool. Observe, and see if you can improve the situation. Dry, brown spots are usually caused by a virus; there is not much you can do. Isolate the plant and do not transfer the disease to your other plants by touching the affected plant and then another. Dry, brown spots on African Violet leaves can be caused by drops of cool water resting on the leaves.

Leaf Reddening – leaves turn red when a plant is placed in light brighter than it is accustomed to. It will pass. Move plant into the light gradually next time.

Brown Leaf Tips – spider plants, particularly, develop dry, brown leaf tips. This is caused by a natural process. To prevent it, wash the tips every morning, or learn to accept it.

Wilting and Darkening – ethylene from wood stoves and fireplaces make plants look wilted and dark and they may die. Cold drafts cause similar effects.

Insect Pests

Some can be destroyed with innocuous remedies, others may only respond to a complete arsenal of noxious chemicals. Pieces missing from plants can usually be traced to greens-crazed pets or carpenters (sow bugs) lurking in the pot until dusk. Prevention is best. If in doubt, throw a plant out.

Common pests include:

- Aphids – small translucent green insects which usually gather on the stems. Isolate the plant to a separate room as aphids can move around. Wash leaves well with soapy water (dishwashing or insecticidal soap). Aphids are usually introduced on plants from the garden or the store or nursery where it was purchased. They can also enter the house on clothes and pets.
- Fungus Gnats – bothersome tiny black flies which swoop around the house at certain times of the year. Their larvae eat fungus in the soil. Pasteurize all soil before using and keep it just moist in spring and autumn. These gnats are a nuisance, but not harmful.
- Mealy Bugs – little grubs in a tuft of white cotton. Dab with a cotton swab soaked in methanol (methyl hydrate or wood alcohol).
- Scale – dark, brown scabs on leaves and stems. Use a cotton swab dipped in methanol to wipe them off. Keep checking the plant for newly hatched scale.

- Spider Mite – small clear or yellow specks all over the leaf and tiny cobwebs on the underside of the leaf. Isolate immediately. I have not found a good remedy, so I throw out the affected plant. This is a common pest, which is usually introduced on purchased plants.
- Whitefly – snow-white flies, tiny in size but big in problems. I spent six months getting rid of them, by hand picking (i.e., crushing every one in sight) every day, from a few plants. The chemicals used for eliminating whitefly are extremely toxic and cannot be used inside a house. I throw out a plant at the first flight of snow. Watch gift plants; poinsettias are notorious for harbouring whitefly.

Types of Houseplants

Many types of plants can be grown inside the house. Most originated in the tropics or subtropics where they grow in a shady location – this is basically the environment in our homes. Years ago people often grew plants that we now grow as garden plants; of course, houses were not well insulated then. The pick-a-back plant, for example, used to be grown in many homes; when I found out that it originated in Siberia, I planted it outside, where it grew well. Many people remember the Spanish shawl houseplant; it is called butterfly flower (*Schizanthus*) in seed catalogues and is grown in greenhouses and in borders. It has wonderful pastel-coloured flowers with intricate patterns and is well worth growing anywhere.

Most houseplants grow well under a range of conditions and it is a matter of observation to determine if they need more or less light, water, and heat. Consult reference books and gardening experts.

Favourite houseplants include:

African Violets – a great favourite, with many shapes and colours of leaves and flowers; they bloom constantly (or they should). Most people start with a store-bought or gift plant, and then they get the "bug," and start trading leaves (see Chapter 12 for propagating method). African Violet seeds are tiny but with care young plants can be raised from seed, providing the seeds are viable. Be prepared to grow many young plants until they flower. Then you can select the ones you like. African Violets grow well in natural or artificial light (see earlier in this chapter and Chapter 12 for techniques). An east-facing window is best, but a south- or west-facing window will do if sheer curtains are drawn when sunlight is intense. If the leaves become pale, they may be getting too much light or not enough fertilizer. If they are not blooming, they may not be getting enough light.

Watering is the usual problem with African Violets. Most people over-water and this rots the roots. Better to err on the side of being a little dry, but do not let them wilt. Overcast, cool days in winter and spring are danger days. Water from the top or bottom? Both methods work. If you water from the bottom regularly, give plants a good watering from the top about once a month as fertilizer salts tend to collect on the surface of the soil and rot the leaf stalks. If you water from the top, use a long-spouted watering can to keep water off the leaves. Droplets of cold water remaining on the leaves cause brown spots. Blotting with paper towels prevents this. African Violets can be washed with a warm spray in the sink and then dried in a warm, draft-free room.

Single or multiple crowns? Single crowns are considered "proper," so pick out the side shoots that come out from the leaves. It is difficult to get your fingers in there, but careful use of a toothpick will snap out the little sprout. Fertilize as for other houseplants. Flowering should be constant and, if it is not, insufficient light is usually the problem if the plant is otherwise healthy. Pick off faded flowers by pulling the flower cluster stalk sideways so that it snaps cleanly from the base of the leaf stalk.

Cacti and Succulents – succulents are adapted to arid regions and store water in their fleshy stems and leaves. Cacti, a type of succulent, usually have spines instead of leaves. All cacti are succulents, but not all succulents are cacti. There are succulent plants in many plant families. There are even succulents on our beaches and cliffs. I grow cacti because most of them have delicate and beautiful flowers that contrast dramatically with the starkness of the plant. Cacti require more attention than other succulents. If you are growing a succulent, approximate the directions outlined (next page) for cacti. Some cacti grow in the blazing tropical sun, others flourish in the shade of trees, shrubs, grass, rocks, or other plants. A few species grow in the cold regions of Alberta; epiphytic species grow on the mossy trunks of trees

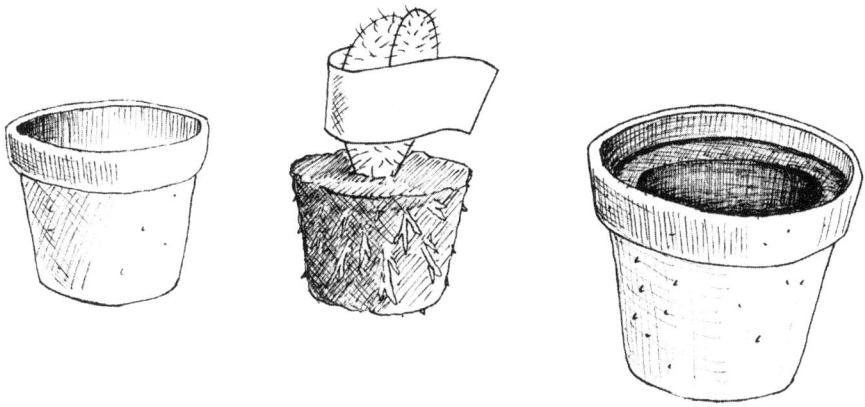

Figure 48. Great care must be taken not to damage a cactus – or yourself – when re-potting.

in tropical or subtropical forests, or on ledges of rock in deep ravines. Holiday cacti (e.g., Christmas cactus) are an example of an epiphytic species. They prefer shade, warmth, humus-rich soil, and adequate moisture.

All cacti require freedom from stagnant moisture. Some grow in poor, dry soil, while others require a rich, loamy soil with abundant water during their growing season. Most cacti have a poorly developed root system so these should not be over-potted (Figure 48), while some, like the Prickly Pear, have an extensive root system. Cacti prefer sunshine, but do not move them suddenly from sun to shade or vice versa. Turn the plants regularly to encourage even growth. Cacti and most succulents do well in a sunny window (southeast- to southwest-facing). I grow my holiday cacti in a northwest-facing window, as they do not like as much light as most cacti.

Potting mixture: use three parts regular potting soil to one part river sand. Planting and re-potting is best done in the spring just as the plant is about to start growth. Pots should not be too large as the root system is small, and too much soil holds too much water for too long. Transplanting can be a prickly affair! Fill the pot with potting mixture and use a pot of the same size as the old one to make a hole. Fold paper towel or newspaper to make a band, wrap it around the plant and use it to handle the plant. This saves both you and the prickles from damage, as they are part of the appeal of this plant. Pack soil around the roots and keep it just moist for a week or two.

Watering: keep the plant relatively dry during the winter and moist from spring to autumn when it is growing. Gradually decrease the amount of water from September onwards.

Growing from seed: use the potting mixture given above. Use a medium pot (4 in / 10 cm) to ensure that the soil does not dry out too quickly. Label the pot. Tamp down the soil. Spread seeds over the surface and cover with 0.25 inches (6 mm) of fine sand. Spray the sand and keep the soil moist. The seeds will germinate in a few days or up to a month or more. Do not despair too soon. Sow seeds at any time, but May-June is good. Grow in seed pot for a year before transplanting. Be careful when watering as they have almost no roots and float up on the water, settle on their sides, and have to be planted again. Bottom watering is better. Do not over-pot when transplanting; it is better to put several in a 3-inch pot.

Rooting cuttings: some cacti form small plantlets which can be separated. Stems of most succulents, pieces of holiday cacti (3-4 segments, cut between segments), or leaves of some succulents (these usually drop leaves when touched) should be allowed to dry for several hours so that the cut surface will heal. Root in moist soil, not covered with a plastic bag, and watch for rot.

Orchids – there are a number of lovely orchids that can be grown in the home. Start out as I suggest and you should have a successful introduction to these beauties. Your first orchids should be blooming-size plants in good health and free of pests and disease. They will cost about $20-25 each. Start with hybrid Cattleyas and relatives (the classic corsage orchids; many colours, many are fragrant) or Phalaenopsis (white or pink Moth Orchid) as these grow well in the home. A south-facing window is best for Cattleyas (leaves are olive green when receiving the right light); Phalaenopsis grows under conditions good for African Violets (leaves should be firm, glossy, and dark green).

Temperature: Phalaenopsis likes warmth, about 70°F (22°C) and Cattleyas prefer warmth by day and cooler at night but not below 50°F (10°C).

Watering: Phalaenopsis needs to be constantly moist, which

is atypical of most orchids; Cattleyas should be watered well when actively growing, indicated by bright green root tips. Do not be alarmed if the roots grow out of the pot. The potting medium should be just moist when they are not actively growing. Fertilize regularly when the plants are growing. Re-potting requires special mixtures of bark chips, available from nurseries where you buy the plants. Do not use soil. Phalaenopsis grows better with a layer of Sphagnum moss spread on top of the bark potting mix.

The plant, however, is the final judge of whether you are treating it properly. Look at your plants and let them tell you that all is not well or that all is wonderful.

Houseplants for Apartments

When college and university students and newly-weds set up housekeeping, they often want some plants in their apartments.

Small plants and cuttings can be acquired from family and friends but there is also the produce counter or the market.

Attractive foliage plants can be grown to a large size quite quickly from seeds removed from tropical fruit. Remove avocado seeds from the fruit and half bury them in a 6-inch (15 cm) pot of soil. They germinate in a few weeks and grow rapidly. Mango seeds should be completely buried. They grow into a small shrub with gracefully drooping leaves of green and bronze.

Other seeds to grow: citrus fruit, pomegranate, and papaya. Grow them in bright light and treat like other houseplants.

"Over-watering is the main problem with houseplants, especially in fall and spring."

Notes

Chapter 14
Arts and Crafts

Many pleasant hours are spent working with the fruits and flowers of your labours. Flowers can be dried and used in their original three-dimensional form for various projects. Dried flowers are used in corsages, table decorations, name tags, gift tags, and wreaths. Flowers can also be pressed flat and used for note cards, pictures, under-the-glass displays of coffee tables or trays, bookmarks, and lampshades.

Drying Flowers

You can grow straw-like flowers like strawflowers and statice; flowers from the garden or roadside also dry reasonably well. The secret is to pick the flowers just after they have started to open, as they will continue to open after being picked. If picked too late, they often go to seed and look unattractive or expel fluffy seeds into the air all winter (a spray of liquid plastic holds these in place). Pick those flowers with sufficient stem for arranging (18 in / 45 cm), strip off all leaves, tie in loose bundles, and hang bundles upside down (Figure 49) in a cool airy place (a basement with good ventilation). Flowers dried in this manner keep much of their colour, although they may darken and lose much of their shape. Grasses are easy to dry and should be picked while green or just as they turn yellowish. Treat as above.

Common flowers which dry well include larkspur, Bells of Ireland, yarrow (cultivated and wild), goldenrod, Joe-Pye-Weed, St. John's wort, ageratum, globe thistle, honesty (money plant, St. Peter's Pennies, etc.), monarda (bee balm), pearly everlasting (wild), hydrangea, red clover, tansy, baby's breath, geranium, ferns (press, see below), Scotch broom, pussy willow, monkshood, marigolds, carnations, and many more, including daffodils.

Sand and cornmeal are sometimes used to dry flowers so that they keep their original three-dimensional shape. I have tried this and it works but, after a while, the flowers absorb moisture from the air and collapse. This is why I recommend the upside-down hanging method outlined above. If you want to dry a large flower, lay it on a piece of paper to dry. It will not remain in its original condition, but it will provide a mass of colour in an arrangement.

Collect plants for drying all through the summer. Do not overlook seed capsules and cones. Even branches and driftwood provide materials for craft and decorating projects.

Berries

For preserving fruit, I use the following recipe: mix one or more parts of the clear part of shellac (let white shellac stand so the white part settles out, then carefully pour off the clear part) to one or less parts of methanol (methyl hydrate, shellac thinners). Cut a long branch containing fruit and remove the leaves. It is best to pick the fruit just after they have turned colour (just ripened). Soak the fruit in the shellac mixture for several hours and drip-dry. The berries often darken and shrivel. Dogberries and northern wild raisin (withrod) are two to try. Rose hips do not require shellac treatment. Attach dried rose hips to a branch to hang in a child's room for a Sugar Plum Tree.

Pressed Flowers

Most flowers can easily be dried by pressing. Use smooth paper towels (those with bumps mar the petals) or newspaper and a large book or catalogue (Figure 50). Small flowers can be pressed whole, but it is best to take apart double flowers like carnations and marigolds and press the petals separately. It takes a week or so for flowers to dry. The pressed flowers and petals are used in many different ways – plaques, pictures, and note cards. Glue in place with white glue and spray or brush on liquid plastic to cover them.

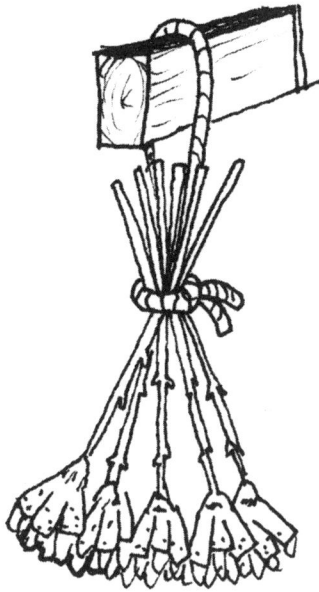

Figure 49. To dry flowers, bundle and hang them upside down in a cool, ventilated room.

Figure 50. Pressing flowers inside a book.

Living Plants

Small potted plants can be used in conjunction with ceramic pieces or in woodworking projects. Make sure they get enough water and light. Some other projects include big bottles planted with small plants, jardinières, hanging fixtures, and anything else that your imagination dictates.

Cut Flowers

Many people enjoy having their own home-grown flowers around the house. A few simple steps ensure that these flowers last as long as possible:

Take a container of clean lukewarm water into the garden with you.

Cut flowers in the cooler part of the day. Check for insects so you do not bring them into the house. I remember a neighbour's experience: an arrangement of dahlias straight from the garden was placed on the table, set for a formal dinner. When she checked the table about ten minutes later, there were earwigs everywhere.

Use sharp clippers to cut flowers with as long a stem as possible. Strip off the lower leaves and put the stems into the water (do not put leaves or flowers into the water).

Leave the flowers in the container in a cool, shady place for several hours or overnight before arranging them.

For woody stems, like lilacs, slit the base of the stem about 0.33 inches (1 cm) up.

"Gardening is a hobby. Never count the cost."

Notes